WHAT YOU NEED TO KNOW ABOUT

HAJJ

Published in the UK by Beacon Books and Media Ltd
Earl Business Centre, Dowry Street, Oldham, OL8 2PF, UK.

www.beaconbooks.net

ISBN: 978-1-915025-53-1 Paperback
ISBN: 978-1-915025-54-8 eBook

Cataloging-in-Publication record for this book is available from the British Library.

Cover design by Raees Mahmood Khan

WHAT YOU NEED TO KNOW ABOUT
HAJJ

BEACON BOOKS

DEDICATION

I begin in the Name of Allah,
the Most Compassionate, the Ever-Merciful.
Dedicated to those who seek the good
pleasure of Allah.

CONTENTS

SPECIAL THANKS TO:

Abdus Salaam for writing this book.

Tahir Mahmood Kiani and Dr. Mostafa Badawi for their editorial support and guidance.

INTRODUCING HAJJ: THE FIFTH PILLAR OF ISLAM

Hajj is the pilgrimage made by Muslims to the Ka'bah in the ancient, holy city of Makkah in Saudi Arabia. The Hajj is the response to the call made by Prophet Ibrahim ﷺ after he and his son, Prophet Isma'il ﷺ, completed the construction of the Ka'bah, the House of Allah. Ever since, pilgrims have continued to visit the Ka'bah for 'Umrah (the minor pilgrimage) and for Hajj (the major pilgrimage). Today, millions of pilgrims continue to respond to the call of Prophet Ibrahim ﷺ and arrive in droves to visit the Ka'bah. Other important areas around Makkah include: Mina, Arafat and Muzdalifah.

There are many other sites to visit and milestones to cross during the Hajj and 'Umrah, which include: circumambulating the Ka'bah, praying near the Maqam Ibrahim (Station of Ibrahim – the place where Prophet Ibrahim ﷺ stood when erecting the Ka'bah) and running (for men, but walking for women) between the hills of Safa and Marwah. Hajj, the major pilgrimage, also includes visiting key landmarks on the outskirts of Makkah, all of which remind pilgrims of pivotal moments in human history and encourage us to reflect upon our own connection with Allah the Most High. The most important day of Hajj is the Day of Arafat because it is the one rite that cannot be dispensed with or substituted, and on this day Allah draws near and asks the angels: "What do these people want?"

Lastly, Hajj is an ancient practice that dates back to Prophet Ibrahim ﷺ and was undertaken by many prophets of old, including the final prophet, Prophet Muhammad ﷺ, who taught mankind the rituals of pilgrimage. The Ka'bah – the focal point of circumambulation for 'Umrah and Hajj – was first built by the angels, before the advent of the first human and prophet, Prophet Adam ﷺ.

WHAT IS HAJJ?

Linguistically, "Hajj" means to intend, realign, or direct oneself towards an object of reverence, veneration, respect, or honour. In Islam, performing Hajj involves undertaking a pilgrimage to Makkah during specific days in the Islamic month of Dhu'l-Hijjah. This pilgrimage includes visiting the Ka'bah – the House of Allah – where pilgrims perform designated acts of worship within a designated period.[1] Dhu'l-Hijjah, the twelfth and final month of the Islamic calendar, follows the lunar cycle. Hajj is observed from the 8th to the 13th of Dhu'l-Hijjah.

A brief summary of these days can be found in the following table:

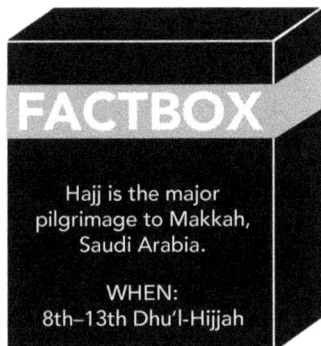

FACTBOX

Hajj is the major pilgrimage to Makkah, Saudi Arabia.

WHEN:
8th–13th Dhu'l-Hijjah

---

1   Ibn Manzur, *Lisan al-'Arab.*

DATE	LOCATION	DURATION	ACTION
8th – 9th	Mina	Arrive on the 8th (preferably before midday). Leave for Arafat on the 9th after sunrise.	Enter ihram (if not already in a state of ihram) and make the intention. Pronounce the talbiyah.
9th	Arafat	Arrive on the 9th after sunrise. Leave for Muzdalifah on the 9th after sunset.	Stay anywhere. Supplicate to Allah.
9th – 10th	Muzdalifah	Arrive on the 9th after sunset. Leave for Mina on the 10th shortly before sunrise.	Collect a minimum of 7 small stones for casting at the Jamrat al-'Aqabah (the large Jamrah) tomorrow, or the maximum of 49 needed for the next few days in Mina.
10th	Mina	Depart for Mina on the 10th.	Cast stones at the Jamrat al-'Aqabah. Sacrifice an animal, unless performing Hajj Ifrad.

DATE	LOCATION	DURATION	ACTION
10th	Makkah	Arrive on or after the 10th.	Cut or shave hair. Exit ihram and wear normal clothes. Circumambulate the Ka'bah 7 times. Perform sa'y between the hills Safa and Marwah.
11th – 12th (13th)	Mina	Arrive on the 11th. Leave on the 12th before sunset or leave on the 13th after midday.	Stone the 3 Jamarat each day after midday.
12th or 13th	Makkah	Arrive on the 12th or 13th.	Perform the Farewell Tawaf.

WHAT ARE THE THREE TYPES OF HAJJ?

Hajj Ifrad: Solitary Hajj
- Enter ihram when Hajj begins.
- Exit ihram when Hajj ends.

Hajj Qir'an: 'Umrah with Hajj
- Enter ihram when 'Umrah begins.
- Exit ihram only after Hajj ends.

Hajj Tamattu': 'Umrah before Hajj
- Enter ihram when 'Umrah begins.
- Exit ihram when 'Umrah ends.
- Enter ihram when Hajj begins.
- Exit ihram when Hajj ends.

Apart from the aforementioned, there are further differences between these three types. One example of a ritual difference between the three types is that Hajj Ifrad does not require a sacrificial animal to complete one's pilgrimage whereas the others (Hajj Qir'an and Hajj Tamattu') do require a sacrificial animal.[2]

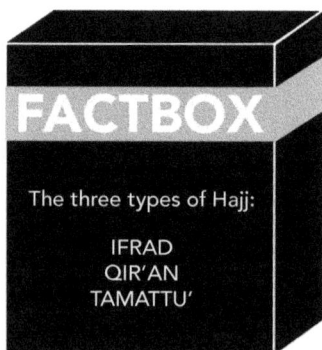

FACTBOX

The three types of Hajj:

IFRAD
QIR'AN
TAMATTU'

---

2 *Hajj and Umrah Made Easy*, (2011), p.6.

WHEN DOES HAJJ BECOME OBLIGATORY?

Hajj becomes obligatory when one is able to financially afford the journey and physically perform it. Pilgrimage to this House, for those who can perform it, is a duty upon people to Allah.[3] When asked what obligates the Hajj on a person, the Holy Prophet Muhammad ﷺ said: "The provisions and a means of conveyance."[4]

The following are the conditions that engender the obligation of Hajj:

- Being Muslim
- Being adult
- Being sane
- Being free
- Having financial security
- Timing of Hajj
- Having means of transport
- Route of Hajj being safe
- Knowledge of Hajj being obligatory
- Having suitable health
- For women: being free of the menstrual cycle and postnatal bleeding

HOW DID THE THREE TYPES OF HAJJ ORIGINATE?

The Prophet Muhammad ﷺ set out for his Farewell Pilgrimage on Saturday 25th February 632 CE[5] [28th Dhu'l-

---

3   Quran, 3:97.
4   At-Tirmidhi, as-Sunan, Hadith 813.
5   Ar-Raheeq al-Makhtum (The Sealed Nectar), Biography of the Noble Prophet, (1996), p.461.

Qa'dah 10 AH]. He set out from Madinah and his only intention was to perform Hajj, not including 'Umrah.

> ... Aishah said: We set out with the Messenger of Allah thinking that it was for nothing other than Hajj.[6]

However, as the Prophet ﷺ was travelling towards Makkah, revelation came that 'Umrah is to be incorporated with Hajj.[7]

> ... Someone came to me tonight from my Lord (Allah) [while I was in the 'Aqiq Valley] and said to me, "Offer ritual prayer in this blessed valley and to assume Ihram for (the performance of) 'Umrah and Hajj together."[8]

The Prophet Muhammad ﷺ embarked on his Farewell Pilgrimage from Madinah on Saturday, February 25 632 CE (28th Dhu'l-Qa'dah 10 AH), with the sole intention of performing Hajj, excluding 'Umrah. Aishah, may Allah be pleased with her, reported that they left with the Prophet ﷺ thinking they were only going to perform Hajj.

As they travelled towards Makkah, a revelation instructed that 'Umrah should be incorporated with Hajj. The Prophet ﷺ received a divine message in the 'Aqiq Valley to offer prayers there and to commence the rites of both 'Umrah and Hajj.

He entered Makkah on March 2 632 CE[9] (4th Dhu'l-Hijjah 10 AH), began the 'Umrah rites, and after

---

6 Al-Nasa'i, Sunan, Hadith 2718.
7 Ar-Raheequl Makhtum (The Sealed Nectar), Biography of the Noble Prophet, (1996), p.462.
8 Al-Bukhari, Sahih, Hadith 1534.
9 Ar-Raheequl Makhtum (The Sealed Nectar), Biography of the Noble Prophet, (1996), p.462.

completing them, he addressed those who had not brought a sacrificial animal. He instructed them to exit their state of ihram, marking the practice of Hajj Tamattu', where pilgrims may temporarily end their ihram after 'Umrah until the Hajj begins. The Prophet ﷺ, having brought a sacrificial animal, continued in his ihram state, which led to the practice of Hajj Qir'an, where the state of ihram is maintained from 'Umrah through Hajj.

Initially intending only to perform Hajj (Hajj Ifrad), the Prophet's journey evolved with the divine guidance to include 'Umrah, leading to a comprehensive demonstration of the three types of Hajj. Pilgrims not carrying a sacrificial animal could conclude their ihram after 'Umrah and re-enter it for Hajj (Hajj Tamattu'), while those like the Prophet ﷺ who brought a sacrificial animal observed Hajj Qir'an, remaining in ihram throughout.

WHAT IS 'UMRAH?

'Umrah is the minor pilgrimage to Makkah, and it consists of fewer rituals than those of Hajj. The rituals of 'Umrah are:[10]

RITUAL	ACTION
Ihram	Wear ceremonial clothing and make intention.
Tawaf	Circumambulate the Ka'bah 7 times, walking the first 3 circuits briskly and in an intimidating manner.
	Attempt to touch the Yemeni Corner.
	Attempt to kiss, touch, or at least indicate towards the al-Hajar al-Aswad with the palms facing it.
Maqam Ibrahim	Pray 2 units of ritual prayer at the Maqam Ibrahim ﷺ.
Sa'y	Walk (men and women) and run (men only) between Mounts Safa and Marwah 7 times.
Shave or trim	Shave or trim the hair and exit ihram clothing.

---

10 *Hajj and Umrah Made Easy,* (2011), pp.14–21.

Please note, since there is a myriad of do's and don'ts, ritual aspects such as supplications, etc. have been purposefully omitted.

In short, the rituals of 'Umrah consist of entering the state of ihram and circumambulating the Ka'bah, as well as attempting to kiss, touch, or indicate towards specific points at the House of Allah. Furthermore, one is to pray at the Maqam Ibrahim, and cross between the two hills of Safa and Marwah. Finally, the pilgrimage ends by the shaving or trimming of hair and exiting the state of ihram by removing the ihram clothing and putting on normal clothing.

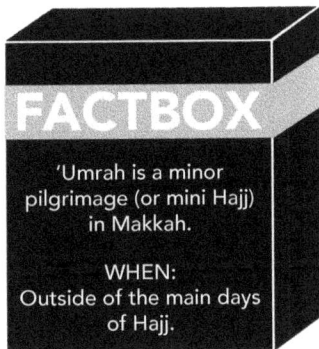

FACTBOX

'Umrah is a minor pilgrimage (or mini Hajj) in Makkah.

WHEN:
Outside of the main days of Hajj.

WHY DO MUSLIMS PERFORM 'UMRAH?

There are a number of reasons why Muslims perform 'Umrah: the primary reason is because it is mentioned in the Quran to do so, though not as an obligation. The secondary reason is because it removes sin. Furthermore, pilgrims also perform 'Umrah in emulation of Prophet Muhammad ﷺ who performed 'Umrah four times after his migration to Madinah.

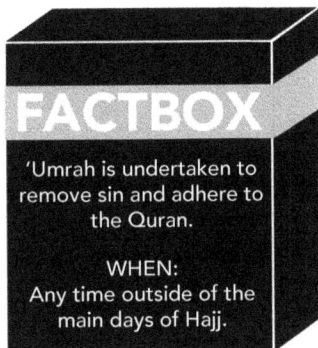

FACTBOX

'Umrah is undertaken to remove sin and adhere to the Quran.

WHEN:
Any time outside of the main days of Hajj.

Ultimately, 'Umrah and Hajj bring peace and tranquillity to worried minds and troubled souls who can find comfort in close proximity to Allah's sanctuary on earth. 'Umrah is therefore an opportunity to seek forgiveness, turn over a new leaf, and start a new chapter in life. It allows people to offload their sorrows and worries and place them all in Allah's Hands, trusting in His decree and Divine Plan.

> *And complete the Hajj and 'Umrah in the service of Allah...*
>
> REFERENCE: QURAN, SURAT AL-BAQARAH, 196

> *... [The performance of] 'Umrah is an expiation for the sins committed between it and the previous one.*
>
> REFERENCE: SAHIH AL-BUKHARI, HADITH NUMBER: 1773

WHAT IS MIQAT?

Miqats are appointed places specified by Prophet Muhammad ﷺ; areas which a pilgrim cannot pass unless he enters into the state of ihram before entering Makkah for pilgrimage. They are geographical markers situated outside of Makkah. Three of the four Miqats are at a distance from Makkah, where a pilgrim reaches and enters into the state of ihram before then travelling towards Makkah. There are five Miqats mentioned by Prophet Muhammad ﷺ.

1. *Miqat Dhu'l-Hulayfah* for people coming from Madinah and the north. Dhu'l-Hulayfah is located 6 miles (10 kms) from Madinah towards the direction of Makkah. This miqat is used by UK travellers visiting Madinah first.

2. *Miqat al-Juhfah* for people coming from or passing through Turkey, Syria, Jordan, Egypt, or Sudan. Al-Juhfah is around 113 miles (182 kms) northwest of Makkah. This miqat is used by UK travellers landing at Jeddah.

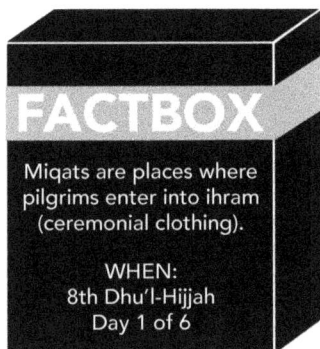

FACTBOX

Miqats are places where pilgrims enter into ihram (ceremonial clothing).

WHEN:
8th Dhu'l-Hijjah
Day 1 of 6

3. *Miqat Qarn al-Manazil* for people coming from or passing through Iraq, Iran, Kuwait, UAE, Oman, or the Najd area. Qarn al-Manazil lies 50 miles (80 kms) east of al-Masjid al-Haram.

4. *Miqat Yalamlam* for people coming from/passing through Yemen and India. Yalamlam is situated approximately 62 miles (100 kms) from al-Masjid al-Haram.

5. *Miqat Dhat 'Irq* is specifically for the people of Iraq. Dhat 'Irq is located around 56 miles (90 kms) northeast of al-Masjid al-Haram.

> *... The Messenger of Allah designated Dhu'l-Hulayfah as the Miqat for the people of Madinah, al-Juhfah for the people of ash-Sham and Egypt, Dhat 'Irq for the people of 'Iraq, Qarn for the people of Najd and Yalamlam for the people of Yemen.*

REFERENCE: SUNAN AL-NASA'I
HADITH NUMBER: 2657, GRADED: SAHIH

Lastly, the Miqat from which Prophet Muhammad ﷺ set out on his Farewell Hajj (Hajjat al-Wada') in 632 CE (10 AH) was Miqat Dhu'l-Hulayfah, as this is the appointed place for the people coming from Madinah. Dhu'l-Hulayfah is also a blessed valley where a masjid known as Masjid Dhu'l-Hulayfah has been constructed, located approximately 7 miles (10 kms) from al-Masjid al-Nabawi.

> *... The Messenger of Allah stayed overnight in Dhu'l-Hulayfah, where he commenced his Hajj...*

REFERENCE: SUNAN AL-NASA'I
HADITH NUMBER: 2660, GRADED: SAHIH

WHAT IS IHRAM?

Ihram is two sheets of unstitched seamless cloth (preferably white but not essential) that men wear during Hajj and 'Umrah. One sheet is wrapped around the lower body, covering the waist downwards, and the other sheet is wrapped around the upper body, placed over the shoulders. This clothing symbolises humility, purity, and equality in mankind. The ihram clothing for women is their usual clothing of modesty and covering. The state of ihram carries some restrictions, such as the prohibition of hunting, shaving the hair and applying perfume, etc.

Ihram is also a "frame of mind" in which focus and thought is directed towards one's intention and the continuous chanting of the Talbiyah.

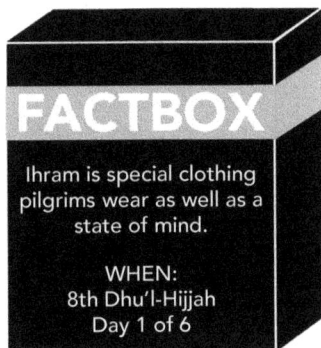

FACTBOX

Ihram is special clothing pilgrims wear as well as a state of mind.

WHEN:
8th Dhu'l-Hijjah
Day 1 of 6

WHAT IS THE TALBIYAH?

The Talbiyah is a special prayer, litany, or call that Muslim pilgrims continuously recite and chant during Hajj or 'Umrah. The Talbiyah is uttered in emulation of Prophet Ibrahim ﷺ, and in mindfulness of Allah the Most High. The Talbiyah of the Messenger of Allah ﷺ was:

لَبَّيْكَ اللّهُمَّ لَبَّيْكَ - لَبَّيْكَ لا شَرِيكَ لَكَ لَبَّيْكَ - إِنَّ الْحَمْدَ
وَالنِّعْمَةَ لَكَ وَالْمُلْكَ - لا شَرِيكَ لَكَ

Labbayka Llahumma Labbayk Labbayka la sharika laka Labbayk Innal hamda wan ni'mata laka wal mulk la sharika lak

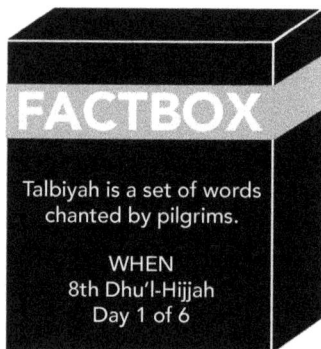

Translation: "Here I am at Your service, O Allah, here I am at Your service. Here I am at Your service. No partner do You have. Here I am at your service. Truly, the praise and the favour are Yours, and the dominion. No partner do You have."

REF: SAHIH AL-BUKHARI
HADITH NUMBER: 1549

ARE THERE VARIATIONS IN THE TALBIYAH?

Yes. There are variations to the Talbiyah whereby some early Muslims would add phrases in addition to the standard recitation made by Prophet Muhammad ﷺ. For example, 'Abdullah ibn 'Umar would add:

$$لَبَّيْكَ اللَّهُمَّ لَبَّيْكَ - لَبَّيْكَ وَسَعْدَيْكَ وَالْخَيْرُ بِيَدَيْكَ وَالرَّغْبَةُ إِلَيْكَ وَالْعَمَلُ$$

Labbayka Llahumma Labbayk Labbayka wa sa'dayka wal-khayru bi-yadayka war-raghbatu ilayka wal-'amal

Translation: "Here I am at Your service, Here I am at Your service. Here I am at Your service; give me blessings, as all good is in Your Hands, all supplications are directed to You, as are all actions."

However, in the modern era it would be unnecessary and uncommon for pilgrims to vary or deviate from the standard recitation of the Talbiyah made by Prophet Muhammad ﷺ.

… The Messenger of Allah began his Talbiyah for Hajj… and some people added [the words]: "Dhu'l-Ma'arij (The Owner of the Pathways to Heaven)" and similar phrases, and the Prophet heard them, and did not say anything.

REF: SUNAN ABU DAWUD
HADITH NUMBER: 1813
GRADED: SAHIH

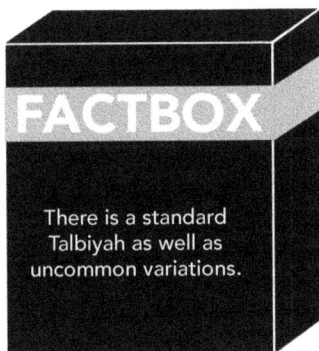

FACTBOX

There is a standard Talbiyah as well as uncommon variations.

The Ka'bah in Makkah, photographed in 1880.

Male pilgrims wearing the Ihram; two sheets of unstitched fabric.

Pilgrims at the Ka'bah in modern-day Makkah.

This is evidence that it is permitted to add words to the Talbiyah though it is not permitted to shorten it.

WHAT ARE THE ORIGINS OF THE TALBIYAH?

The chanting of the Talbiyah is a response to a call that Prophet Ibrahim ﷺ made. When he had completed the construction of the Ka'bah, he said: "O Lord, how can I convey this to people when my voice will not reach them?" It was said: "Call them and We will convey it." So, Prophet Ibrahim ﷺ climbed Mount Abu Qubays [in Makkah] and said, "O mankind! Your Lord has established a House so come for pilgrimage to it." It is said that the mountains lowered themselves so that his voice would reach all the regions of the earth, and those who were still in their mother's womb and their father's loin would hear the call. The response came from everyone in the cities, deserts and countryside, and everyone whom Allah has decreed will make the pilgrimage until the Day of Resurrection. It is said everyone on earth received the call, including those who were not yet born.

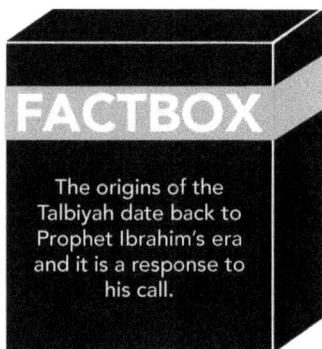

FACTBOX

The origins of the Talbiyah date back to Prophet Ibrahim's era and it is a response to his call.

And call the people to Hajj, and they shall come to you on foot and mounted on every lean camel – coming from every faraway route.

REFERENCE: QURAN
SURAT AL-HAJJ, 27

WHAT IS TAWAF?

Tawaf is to circumambulate the Ka'bah seven times. The first three circuits are walked in haste with the shoulders swinging from side to side (this is specific to men), whilst the remaining four circuits are walked at a normal pace. During the circumambulation of the Ka'bah, one attempts to touch the Yemeni Corner and kiss or touch the al-Hajar al-Aswad, or at least indicate towards it. Tawaf around the Ka'bah has been described as salah (ritual prayer), except that one is permitted to talk during it.

... Tawaf around the House is similar to ritual prayer (salah) except that you may talk during it. So, whoever talks in it, then let him say nothing but good.

REFERENCE: TIRMIDHI
HADITH NUMBER: 960
GRADED: HASAN

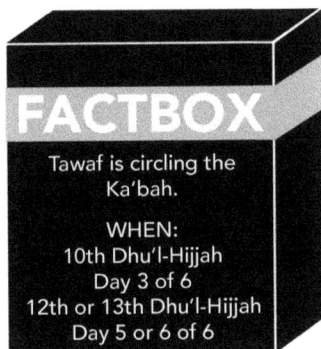

FACTBOX

Tawaf is circling the Ka'bah.

WHEN:
10th Dhu'l-Hijjah
Day 3 of 6
12th or 13th Dhu'l-Hijjah
Day 5 or 6 of 6

WHY ARE THE FIRST THREE CIRCUITS DONE IN A HURRIED MANNER (RAMAL)?

The brisk pace and intimidating manner of the first three circuits of Tawaf is called "Ramal". The reason one does Ramal is to demonstrate physical strength. The origins of Ramal date back to March 629 CE [Dhu'l-Qa'dah 7 AH] when the Prophet Muhammad ﷺ returned to Makkah from exile, and he was briefly allowed to perform 'Umrah because of the Hudaybiyyah Peace Treaty, which was signed in the previous year. The Muslims came to perform 'Umrah in Makkah and were weakened by fever, but Prophet Muhammad ﷺ did not want to show weakness in front of his foes. The Muslims thus performed Tawaf in a brisk manner: short quick steps, chest out, and moving the shoulders firmly from side to side, instead of conventional walking. They demonstrated strength towards an enemy that thought the Muslims had become weak.

The Messenger of Allah and his Companions came to Makkah, and they had been weakened by the fever of Yathrib. The idolators said: "Tomorrow there will come to you people who have been weakened by fever and they have suffered greatly because of it..."

REFERENCE: SAHIH MUSLIM
HADITH NUMBER: [3059] 240 – (1266)

... Your people will see you tomorrow, so let them see you looking strong...

REFERENCE: SUNAN IBN MAJAH
HADITH NUMBER: 2953, GRADED: HASAN

The polytheists of Makkah sat on Mount Qu'ayqi'an and watched the Muslims performing Tawaf, expecting to see weakness. When they saw the Muslims running briskly around the Ka'bah on three sides (because the fourth side was concealed by the Ka'bah), they were in awe of their strength. They later remarked:

... These people whom you said had been weakened by fever are stronger than such-and-such...

REFERENCE: SAHIH MUSLIM
HADITH NUMBER: [3059] 240 – (1266)

... It is as if they are gazelles!

REFERENCE: SUNAN ABU DAWUD
HADITH NUMBER: 1889, GRADED: HASAN

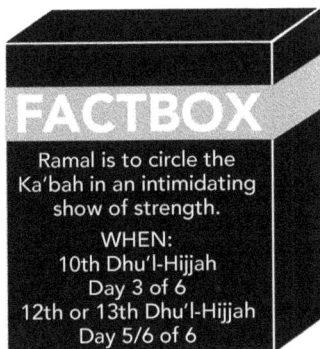

FACTBOX

Ramal is to circle the Ka'bah in an intimidating show of strength.

WHEN:
10th Dhu'l-Hijjah
Day 3 of 6
12th or 13th Dhu'l-Hijjah
Day 5/6 of 6

WHAT IS THE YEMENI CORNER?

The Ka'bah has four corners in total, two of which are named the Yemeni Corner. As Yemen is situated towards the south of the Ka'bah, the two south-facing corners – where the al-Hajar al-Aswad is placed and the Yemeni Corner is – are both called "Yemeni Corners". However, the second Yemeni Corner, where the al-Hajar al-Aswad (Black Stone) is affixed, is more commonly known as the "al-Hajar al-Aswad Corner". The other two north-facing corners of the Ka'bah are called Iraqi and Shami because they face towards Iraq and Syria respectively.

Pilgrims attempt to touch the Yemeni corners to emulate the Prophet Muhammad ﷺ, who would touch both the al-Hajar al-Aswad and the Yemeni Corner in each of his circuits while circumambulating the Ka'bah.

FACTBOX

The Yemeni Corner is an unsheathed corner of the Ka'bah which pilgrims attempt to touch.

This is among the sacred places where prayers are answered.

... The Messenger of Allah would never omit touching the Yemeni Corner and the al-Hajar al-Aswad in each of his circuits...

REFERENCE: SUNAN ABU DAWUD
HADITH NUMBER: 1876, GRADED: HASAN

... I did not see the Messenger of Allah touch any but the two Yemeni Corners.

REFERENCE: SAHIH MUSLIM
HADITH NUMBER: [3066] 247 – (1269)

The Holy Prophet Muhammad ﷺ is reported to have said: "Touching the al-Hajar al-Aswad and the Yemeni Corner indeed erases sins."

... I heard Ibn Hisham asking 'Ata bin Abu Rabah about the Yemenite Corner, when he was performing Tawaf around the House. 'Ata said: Abu Hurayrah told me that the Prophet said: "Seventy angels have been appointed over it. Whoever says the following, they say: Ameen"...

اللّهُمَّ إِنِّي أَسْأَلُكَ الْعَفْوَ وَالْعَافِيَةَ فِي الدُّنْيَا وَالآخِرَةِ رَبَّنَا آتِنَا فِي الدُّنْيَا حَسَنَةً وَفِي الْآخِرَةِ حَسَنَةً وَقِنَا عَذَابَ النَّارِ

Allahumma inni 'as'alukal-'afwa wal-'aafiyata fi'd dunya wal-akhirah Rabbana aatina fi'd-dunya hasanatan wa fi'l-akhirati hasanatan waqina 'adhaaban-naar

Translation: "O Allah, I ask You for pardon and well-being in this world and in the Hereafter. Our Lord, give us good in this world, good in the Hereafter, and protect us from the torment of the Fire."

REFERENCE: SUNAN IBN MAJAH
HADITH NUMBER: 2957, GRADED: DA'IF

In short: Prophet Muhammad ﷺ would touch both the Yemeni corner and al-Hajar al-Aswad in each of his Tawaf circuits around the Ka'bah. This is the reason why both of these – the Yemeni Corner and the al-Hajar al-Aswad – are left exposed and uncovered.

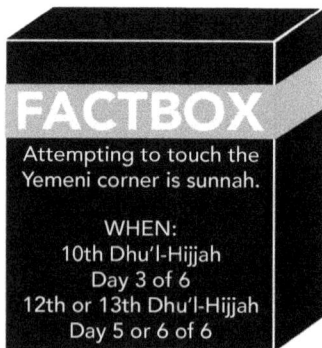

FACTBOX

Attempting to touch the Yemeni corner is sunnah.

WHEN:
10th Dhu'l-Hijjah
Day 3 of 6
12th or 13th Dhu'l-Hijjah
Day 5 or 6 of 6

WHAT IS THE AL-HAJAR AL-ASWAD (BLACK STONE)?

The al-Hajar al-Aswad (Black Stone) is a stone that descended from heaven and is located at one corner of the Ka'bah. This corner is known as al-Hajar al-Aswad – al-Rukn an-Aswad (The Black [Stone] Corner). Pilgrims attempt to touch al-Hajar al-Aswad because it absorbs their sins. Initially, the stone was white but blackened with time due to it absorbing the sins "off from those who touched it".

… Al-Hajar al-Aswad descended from Paradise, and it was whiter than milk, then it was blackened by the sins of the children of Adam.

REFERENCE: TIRMIDHI
HADITH NUMBER: 877
GRADED: HASAN

FACTBOX

Brought from Paradise, al-Hajar al-Aswad (Black Stone) is a stone that absorbs the sins of those that kiss it, touch it, or indicate towards it.

It goes without saying that al-Hajar al-Aswad (or the Ka'bah for that matter) is not to be worshipped, for worship is only for Allah. Allah is the

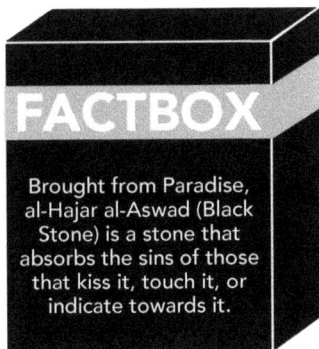

ultimate forgiver of sins but al-Hajar al-Aswad will testify on the Day of Resurrection for those who kiss it, touch it, or indicate towards it. Nonetheless, the ultimate forgiveness of all sin – after its testimony – still rests with Allah.

> *...Allah will raise [al-Hajar al-Aswad] on the Day of Resurrection with two eyes by which it sees, and a tongue that it speaks with, testifying to whoever indicated towards it in true faith.*

REFERENCE: TIRMIDHI
HADITH NUMBER: 961, GRADED: HASAN

'Umar ؓ understood the ultimate forgiver of sins is Allah the Most High, and al-Hajar al-Aswad cannot erase sin unless Allah Himself forgives. Nonetheless, 'Umar ؓ still kissed al-Hajar al-Aswad because Prophet Muhammad ﷺ did so.

> *... I saw 'Umar kissing al-Hajar al-Aswad and clinging to it, and he said: "I saw the Messenger of Allah having much honour for you."*

REFERENCE: SAHIH MUSLIM
HADITH NUMBER: [3071] 252 – (1271)

Kissing it, touching it, or indicating towards it (if the first two are not possible) is to symbolise one's fealty to Allah, the Lord of the worlds.

Istilam is the act of kissing al-Hajar al-Aswad by placing one's hands on either side of it. If this is not possible for any reason, then one should touch it with their hands and then kiss their hands. If this too is not possible, then one should raise their hands – facing their palms towards al-Hajar al-Aswad as if placing their hands on it – and then kiss their hands.

Ibn 'Umar ؓ reported: "I have seen the Holy Prophet ﷺ perform istilam and kiss it."

THE ORIGINS OF AL-HAJAR AL-ASWAD

When Prophet Ibrahim ﷺ was building the Ka'bah, one more stone was needed. His son Isma'il ﷺ wanted to go and get something, but Prophet Ibrahim ﷺ said, "Help me to find a stone as I told you to do." So, Isma'il ﷺ set out looking for a stone, but when he brought it to his father, he found that his father had already set al-Hajar al-Aswad in place. He asked, "Dear father, who brought you this stone?" He replied, "It was brought to me by one who is not relying on you to build it. It was brought to me by Jibril ﷺ from heaven."

The al-Hajar al-Aswad was originally a single piece of rock but, due to various incidents that occurred throughout history, it today consists of several pieces of different sizes that have been joined together. They are surrounded by a silver frame which is fastened by silver nails to the outer wall of the Ka'bah, approximately 150 centimetres from the ground. The original silver frame was built by 'Abdullah ibn Zubayr and was later replaced by other rulers as and when the need arose.

The exposed face of al-Hajar al-Aswad currently measures approximately 20 centimetres (7.9 inches) by 16 centimetres (6.3 inches). Its

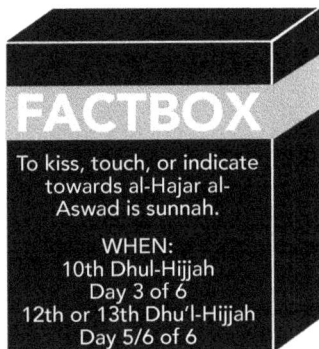

FACTBOX

To kiss, touch, or indicate towards al-Hajar al-Aswad is sunnah.

WHEN:
10th Dhul-Hijjah
Day 3 of 6
12th or 13th Dhu'l-Hijjah
Day 5/6 of 6

original size is uncertain and the recorded dimensions have changed considerably over time, as the setting for the fragments has been remodelled on several occasions.

WHAT IS THE KA'BAH?

The Ka'bah is the first building dedicated to the worship of Allah for mankind. The Ka'bah is an empty "cube-shaped stone building" located within the open courtyard of the al-Masjid al-Haram (the Sacred Masjid) in Makkah. It is commonly referred to as the "House of God". It is the focal point towards which all Muslims face in their five daily prayers and pilgrims circumambulate.

WHY IS IT CALLED KA'BAH?

The reason it is called Ka'bah is because it is muka'ab, i.e. in the shape of a cube (ka'b). It is also called Ka'bah because it is cubic (murabba'). In essence, it is called Ka'bah because of its shape and no other reason, although in actuality its shape is more rectangular than cube.

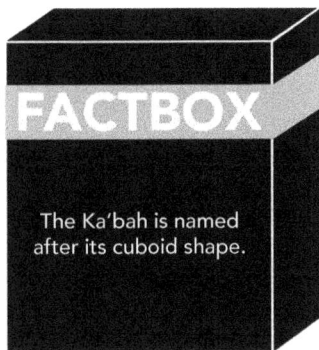

FACTBOX

The Ka'bah is named after its cuboid shape.

WHO BUILT AND REBUILT THE KA'BAH?

The Ka'bah was originally built by the angels two thousand years prior to the creation of Prophet Adam ﷺ. It was later rebuilt by Prophet Adam ﷺ and then by Prophet Sheeth ﷺ after the Great Flood of Prophet Nuh ﷺ.

Prophet Ibrahim ﷺ used to travel from Palestine to visit his wife Hajar and his son Prophet Isma'il ﷺ, and it was on his third visit that he informed Prophet Isma'il of Allah's command to rebuild the Ka'bah, and so it was reconstructed by them both about four thousand years ago. It was then rebuilt by the 'Amaliqah tribe, followed by a reconstruction by the Jurhum tribe. After them, Qusayy ibn Kilab rebuilt the Ka'bah. It was later rebuilt by the Quraish tribe during the lifetime of and also by Prophet Muhammad ﷺ himself.

After this, it has also been occasionally re-built again as and when maintenance was needed. For example, it was reconstructed by Abdullah ibn Zubayr, then by Hajjaj ibn Yusuf, and most recently (albeit over a thousand years ago), by Sultan Murad Khan 'Uthmani. The Ka'bah was damaged due to natural disasters and even due to attacks by the enemy which required its reconstruction on the same spot a number of times.

The Ka'bah has been a place of worship since it was first built by the angels. 'Ali ibn Husayn (also known as Imam Zayn al-Abidin) was

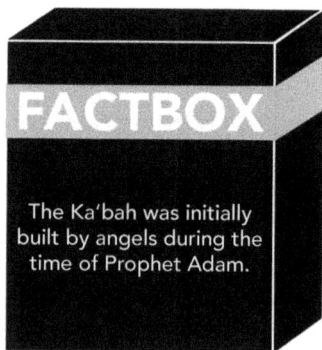

asked, "Since when has the circumambulation of the Ka'bah been performed?" He replied, "[Since the time] when Allah informed His angels about appointing His vicegerent on earth, and they remarked, 'We glorify You and praise You. Will you place on earth humans as Your vicegerents, those who will spread mischief and corruption on the earth, and who will shed blood?' Allah replied, 'You do not know what I know.' As a consequence, the angels felt extremely ashamed of their questioning, and so out of remorse and humility they circumambulated the 'Arsh (Divine Throne) thrice. Bestowing His special mercy upon them, Allah created the Bayt al-Ma'mur below the 'Arsh and said, 'Circumambulate this [House].' Each day, 70,000 angels circumambulate it, and once an angel visits it, they never get an opportunity to visit it again.

Then Allah said to the angels, 'Build Me a House on earth of its likeness and proportions.' When the sanctified House was built, the creatures of the earth were commanded, 'They must circumambulate this House like the inhabitants of the heavens circumambulate the Bayt al-Ma'mur.'"

Bayt al-Ma'mur, which is mentioned in the Quran (52:4), is the Ka'bah of the angels in the seventh heaven, directly above the Ka'bah.

ORIGINS OF THE KA'BAH

> ... The Hour will not begin... until the land of the Arabs goes back to being meadows with rivers.

Makkah was once lush and green with a healthy population, but eventually became a desert when the rivers dried up and the meadows turned to sand. It then became difficult for humans to inhabit this area. Many, many years later, approximately 4,000 years ago when Prophet Isma'il ﷺ was born, Allah revealed to Prophet Ibrahim ﷺ that he should take his wife Hajar and baby Isma'il ﷺ to Makkah.

Later, Prophet Ibrahim ﷺ with the help of his son, rebuilt the Ka'bah, and they did so in the middle of the valley surrounded by hills. Prophet Isma'il ﷺ collected the rocks which Prophet Ibrahim ﷺ used for its construction.

DESCRIPTION OF THE KA'BAH

- The current height of the Ka'bah is 13.1 metres (43 feet), the width is just over 11 metres (36 feet), and the length is almost 13 metres (42 feet).
- The al-Hajar al-Aswad is located on the Ka'bah's eastern corner. It is the spot where Muslims start and end their circumambulation of the Ka'bah. The al-Hajar al-Aswad is placed inside a pure silver frame and affixed to the eastern corner of the Ka'bah.
- The 300 kg (660 lb) gold doors of the Ka'bah are set 213 centimetres (7 feet) above the ground on the north-eastern wall of the Ka'bah between the al-Hajar al-Aswad corner and the Iraqi corner – closer to the former. The top of these doors is 5.5 metres (18 feet) above the ground.
- The interior of the Ka'bah is 220 centimetres

higher than the Tawaf area outside, with a single chamber, having three brown wooden pillars (each almost 1,400 years old, with a perimeter of 150 centimetres and a diameter of 44 centimetres) supporting the roof, and its interior walls are lined with green coloured cloth and white marble tiles. Its floor is also covered in white marble tiles with a border of green marble tiles. There is a distinctive mark on the floor opposite the door of the Ka'bah where the Holy Prophet Muhammad ﷺ is reported to have performed ritual prayer.

- The Hijr/Hatim is a low curved wall along the outside of the north-western wall of the Ka'bah, which was part of the original Ka'bah.
- The Mizab al-Rahmah (Spout of Mercy) is the edge of the Ka'bah inside the Hatim area of the north-western wall of Ka'bah, from where rainwater overflows onto the ground of the Hatim. A rain spout was added to aid the flow of water, and a spout made of gold was added to the Ka'bah in 1627 CE. This is among the sacred places where prayers are answered.
- Al-Multazam (Place of Attachment) is the portion of the north-eastern wall of the Ka'bah, approximately 2 metres (6 feet 6 inches) of space, between the al-Hajar al-Aswad and the door of the Ka'bah. Al-Multazam is among the sacred places where prayers are answered.
- Al-Mustajab (Place of Acceptance) is the south-eastern wall of the Ka'bah – between the Yemeni Corner and al-Hajar al-Aswad Corner – where 70,000 angels are appointed, proclaiming "Ameen" to the supplications made there.

Al-Hajar al-Aswad, or Black Stone, is a stone sent from heaven.

The Maqam Ibrahim in the foreground with the Ka'bah in the background. The Ka'bah's Mizab al-Rahmah (Spout of Mercy) is also visible.

- Al-Mustajar is the portion of the south-western wall of the Ka'bah – between the al-Shami Corner and the Yemeni Corner – directly opposite the al-Multazam.
- Musalla Jibril is the place where the Angel Jibril ﷺ is reported to have shown the Holy Prophet Muhammad ﷺ how to perform the obligatory ritual prayer at the five different times of the day. The Musalla Jibril is located on the ground at the bottom right side of the door to the Ka'bah. It is marked by 8 small pieces of brown marble of different sizes affixed to a white marble tile sloping downwards from the Ka'bah.
- Al-Kiswah is the cloth covering the Ka'bah. Currently in black silk and embroidered with Arabic calligraphy of Quranic verses in gold thread, it used to be of different colours in the past, including red and white stripes, completely white, red brocade, yellow brocade, and green. Al-Kiswah covers 658 square metres and weighs 570 kg, with 15 kg of gold threads. It is changed annually.

WHAT IS THE HIJR/HATIM?

The Hijr, also known as the Hatim, is an area that is currently demarcated by a short, curved wall next to the cubed edifice of the Ka'bah. This area was once part of the Ka'bah itself but was excluded from the building when the Quraish rebuilt the House. Prophet Muhammad ﷺ was thirty-five years old and hadn't yet declared Prophethood when the Ka'bah was being rebuilt at this time.

WHY WAS THE HIJR/HATIM EXCLUDED FROM THE KA'BAH?

During the lifetime of Prophet Muhammad ﷺ and before the Divine Revelation began, the Ka'bah was in need of structural maintenance. So, the Quraish planned to rebuild the House. The Quraish wanted to rebuild the House with "pure" money only so they refused to accept funds

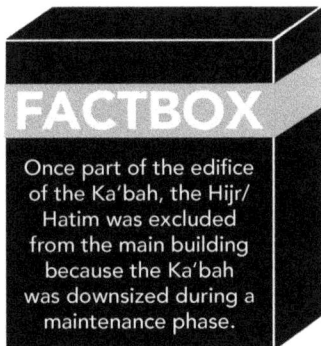

FACTBOX

Once part of the edifice of the Ka'bah, the Hijr/Hatim was excluded from the main building because the Ka'bah was downsized during a maintenance phase.

from prostitution, usury, extortion or other unfair and illicit means. However, they fell short of the necessary funds and building material, because of which they re-built the Ka'bah smaller in size, and the area left outside of the building is now called the Hijr or Hatim, and it demarcates the original boundary.

The curved wall that demarcates the Hijr/Hatim is cov-ered in white marble, and is approximately 150 centime-tres high and 90 centimetres wide.

- Abdul Muttalib, the grandfather of the Prophet Muhammad ﷺ, loved to sit at this place. It was here that he had a dream in which the Zamzam well was disclosed to him, which until then had been buried since the time of the Jurhum tribe.
- This is also the place where the Isra' (Night Journey) and Mi'raj (Heavenly Ascension) of the Prophet Muhammad ﷺ began.
- Additionally, it is the place where the Prophet Muhammad ﷺ came when the people did not believe him about the Isra' and Mi'raj, and Allah displayed the Bayt al-Maqdis in front of him, and he described it to them as he looked at it.
- Prophet Isma'il ﷺ is buried here, together with his mother, Hajar.

WHY DO PILGRIMS PRAY INSIDE THE HIJR/HATIM?

The reason pilgrims pray inside the Hijr/Hatim is because it is equivalent to praying inside the Ka'bah itself, as this area was once part of the House of Allah. Nevertheless, praying inside the Hijr/Hatim is not part of the Hajj or

'Umrah ritual but something optional, i.e. if one desires to do so.

However, when circumambulating the Ka'bah during Hajj or 'Umrah, one must not cross through the Hjir/Hatim otherwise that circuit would be deemed incomplete. The circumambulation must be performed outside of the Hajir/Hatim.

> *Aishah narrated: "I wanted to enter the House to perform ritual prayer in it, so the Messenger of Allah took me by the hand and led me inside the Hijr, and he said: 'Perform ritual prayer in the Hijr if you want to enter the House, for indeed it is part of the House, but your people considered it insignificant when they built the Ka'bah, so they left it outside of the House.'"*

REFERENCE: TIRMIDHI
HADITH NUMBER: 876, GRADED: SAHIH

The inside of the Ka'bah is among the sacred places where prayers are answered, which would also include the Hatim.

WHAT IS THE MAQAM IBRAHIM?

The Maqam Ibrahim is a black-reddish stone with hints of white near the Ka'bah, which has the footprints of Prophet Ibrahim ﷺ.

According to one tradition, it appeared when Prophet Ibrahim ﷺ stood on the stone while building the Ka'bah. When the walls became too high, Prophet Ibrahim ﷺ stood on the stone, which miraculously rose up to let him continue building and also miraculously lowered down in order to allow Prophet Isma'il ﷺ to hand him the stones.

The stone inside the casing is square-shaped and measures 40 centimetres (16 inches) in length and width, and 20 centimetres (approx. 8 inches) in height. Currently, it is placed inside a golden metal enclosure. The outer casing has changed a number of times over the years. The length of the footprints is 20 centimetres, and their depth is 9-10 centimetres.

The stone of Maqam Ibrahim, inside its enclosure, is situated 43 feet (approximately 13 metres) in front of the door of the Ka'bah, between the al-Hajr al-Aswad corner and the Iraqi corner. Most people try to gain a place to face this enclosure towards the Ka'bah when performing the two units of ritual prayer after having completed the circumambulation. However, if someone cannot find space here, they may offer their two units anywhere within the Tawaf area (mataf).

Currently, the actual footprints of the Maqam Ibrahim are covered up. A silver alloy case with two deep imprints of feet is what is visible, and the original footprints can no longer be seen.

A point to note is that although the pre-Islamic polytheistic Arabs worshipped stones during the Age of Ignorance (Jahiliyyah), no one ever worshipped the al-Hajar al-Aswad or the Maqam Ibrahim, even though they held them in high regard. It appears that it was Allah's will to protect these two stones from all types of worship.

Moreover, the Maqam Ibrahim is a place for the performance of ritual prayer and not for touching or kissing. When the area is crowded, it is better to perform ritual prayer some distance away from the Maqam Ibrahim to avoid causing unnecessary inconvenience to oneself and to others.

The Maqam Ibrahim is among the sacred places where prayers are answered.

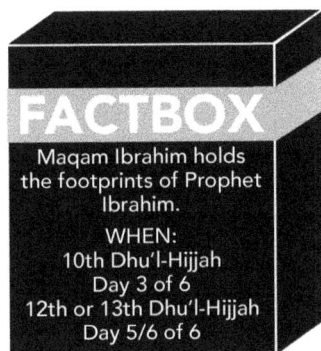

FACTBOX

Maqam Ibrahim holds the footprints of Prophet Ibrahim.

WHEN:
10th Dhu'l-Hijjah
Day 3 of 6
12th or 13th Dhu'l-Hijjah
Day 5/6 of 6

... When the walls became high, Isma'il brought this stone and placed it for Prophet Ibrahim who stood over it and carried on building...

REFERENCE: SAHIH AL-BUKHARI, HADITH NUMBER: 3364

During the lifetime of Prophet Muhammad ﷺ and Abu Bakr ◈, this stone was attached to the Ka'bah, but then Umar ◈ moved it to its current location so as to make it easy for people to pray next to the Maqam.

... Now make the place, where Ibrahim stood into a place of ritual prayer.

REFERENCE: QURAN, AL-BAQARAH, 125

WHAT IS AS-SAFA WA'L-MARWAH?

Safa and Marwah are two hills in Makkah, and they are situated in close proximity to the Ka'bah. Safa is situated south of the Ka'bah, and it is the point where the sa'y (walk) begins. Marwah is north-east of the Ka'bah.

Both of these mounts are now covered due to the extensions made to the al-Masjid al-Haram complex, but can still be seen: Safa, behind a glass screen, and Marwah, beneath a transparent resin. There are ramps going up to both these mounts.

Men who perform 'Umrah or Hajj should both walk and run (but women should only walk), seven times between these two hills. The history of Mounts Safa and Marwah is intertwined with the unearthing of water through the discovery of the Zamzam spring.

Mounts Safa and Marwah are among the sacred places

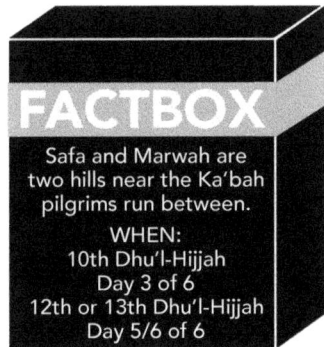

FACTBOX

Safa and Marwah are two hills near the Ka'bah pilgrims run between.

WHEN:
10th Dhu'l-Hijjah
Day 3 of 6
12th or 13th Dhu'l-Hijjah
Day 5/6 of 6

where prayers are answered, especially when performing the sa'y between them.

> *Mounts Safa and Marwah are among Allah's (sacred) symbols.*

REFERENCE: QURAN, SURAT AL-BAQARAH, 158
TRANSLATED BY: TAHIR MAHMOOD KIANI

Zamzam is a sacred well located 20 metres to the east of the Ka'bah, in the courtyard of the al-Masjid al-Haram. The water from the well is also called Zamzam.

In the current era, the well is covered so one cannot see nor access it; instead, the water is carried through pipes into faucets. The sacred well was discovered by Lady Hajar when Prophet Ibrahim عليه السلام left her alone in the wilderness and baby Isma'il عليه السلام, with only some dates and a small water-skin filled with water. This took place approximately 4,000 years ago.

When Isma'il عليه السلام was born, Allah revealed to Prophet Ibrahim عليه السلام that he should take his wife Hajar and baby Isma'il عليه السلام to Makkah. Prophet Ibrahim عليه السلام left Hajar and Isma'il alone in the wilderness – where Makkah is situated today – and supplicated to Allah:

> *O our Lord! Verily, I have settled my offspring [Isma'il (Ishmael)] in the barren valley [of Makkah] in the close vicinity of Your Sacred House, O our Lord, so that they may establish Prayer. So, make the hearts of the people incline towards them with love and fondness, and provide for them [all kinds of] fruits as sustenance so that they may remain grateful.*

REFERENCE: QURAN, SURAH IBRAHIM, 37
TRANSLATED BY: DR. MUHAMMAD TAHIR-UL-QADRI

Hajar عليها السلام anxiously waited with Isma'il عليه السلام in the desert. She suckled him and drank the water she had. When the water finished, she began to panic. She ran to and fro between the two hills of Safa and Marwah in the hope of seeing somebody who could help. There was nobody in sight, but a quiet voice spoke, and then she saw an angel digging the Zamzam well until water began to flow. It is said Hajar gathered (zummat) sand around the water as it gushed because she feared that Isma'il عليه السلام would be harmed by the immense rush of water, so she exclaimed, "Zam! Zam! (Stop! Stop!)" Thereafter, the pressure of the surging water eased. It has since been referred to as Zamzam. The water attracted the Jurhum tribe who later settled in the city of Makkah.

- Zamzam water is unlike conventional water, as it is high in minerals and radiological features, and shows the potential to cure numerous diseases.
- Prayers are answered when drinking Zamzam water.
- On the virtues of Zamzam water, the Prophet Muhammad ﷺ said: "The water of Zamzam is for whatever [intention] it is drunk."
- At the beginning of the Night Journey and Heavenly Ascension of the Prophet Muhammad ﷺ (al-Isra' wa al-Mi'raj), the angels washed his heart with Zamzam water.

CURRENT STATE OF THE ZAMZAM WELL

The Zamzam well used to be accessible to the general public, but then it was covered and only made available to people using stairs in a basement near the

Ka'bah. It is now completely covered by the circumambulation area and not accessible to the general public. Its water is drawn using electric pumps and motors, which is stored in water tanks and coolers for people to drink from. Water distribution centres have also been placed in various areas around al-Masjid al-Haram for easy access for the worshippers.

According to a report published in 2023, the amount of water pumped per day is 150,000 litres at an average of 11 litres per second, the maximum of which is 18.5 litres per second. In 2010, the annual limit on how much water could be extracted from the well was stated as c. 500,000 cubic meters (700,000 cu. yd), though due to annual variations in rainfall patterns there exists a lot of variation with regards to how much water can be extracted without lowering the well's water level too drastically each year.

The Zamzam spring has been providing water for over 5,000 years. 120 tonnes of Zamzam water is transported on a daily basis to the tanks al-Masjid al-Nabawi in Madinah through truck tankers with special instructions to protect the water from any damage. Zamzam water is provided in 7,000 sterile containers and distributed inside and around al-Masjid al-Nabawi.

Every year, millions of pilgrims visit this place and drink Zamzam water to their fill, and they also take plenty of it home with them for their own

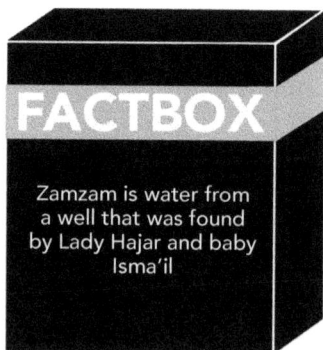

FACTBOX

Zamzam is water from a well that was found by Lady Hajar and baby Isma'il

drinking purposes and to share with others. It is also sent all over the world for Muslims to consume.

WHY DO PILGRIMS WALK AND RUN BETWEEN THE HILLS SAFA AND MARWAH?

Walking and running (for men only) between these two hills/mounts is called sa'y. The reason pilgrims walk and run between them is:

1) To remember the search of Hajar ﷺ who ran between these hills looking for water.

2) To remember the running of Prophet Ibrahim ﷺ who escaped from Iblis.

3) To remember the walk and run of Prophet Muhammad ﷺ who marched to and fro in front of his polytheist foes.

The place between these mounts where the sa'y takes place is known as the mas'a, and today, green lights mark the beginning and the ending of the running portion.

Al-Kiswah, or textile cover of the Ka'bah, is adorned with Islamic inscriptions calligraphed in Arabic with golden threads.

The curved wall of the Hijr/Hatim was once part of the Ka'bah's structure.

Maqam Ibrahim, which holds the blessed footprints of Prophet Ibrahim.

The hill of Safa and below, the hill of Marwah.

المـروة
نهاية الشوط
End of Saee
سعي ختم

Pilgrims performing sa'y, walking or running between both hills.

WHAT IS MINA?

Mina is an open and rugged plot of land that is situated 5 miles (8 kilometres) to the east of Makkah. It is an essential place to visit during the Hajj. Mina is among the sacred places where prayers are answered.

WHAT RITUALS OCCUR AT MINA?

At Mina, pilgrims cast small stones or pebbles at three stone pillars which represent Shaytan, the Devil. Shaytan is pelted to remember his attempt at misleading Isma'il ﷺ on the day Prophet Ibrahim ﷺ attempted to sacrifice his son upon divine instruction. The ritual of sacrificing an animal occurs on the 10th of Dhu'l-Hijjah to commemorate the symbolic sacrifice of Isma'il ﷺ as carried out by Prophet Ibrahim ﷺ.

FACTBOX

Pilgrims camp at Mina, pelt the Devil and offer their sacrificial animal.

WHEN:
8th, 10th & 11th
Dhu'l-Hijjah
Day 1, 3 & 4 of 6

The pilgrims of Hajj stay in Mina on the 8th, 10th and 11th of Dhu'l-Hijjah, spending their time in recitation of the Quran, praying, and supplicating to Allah.

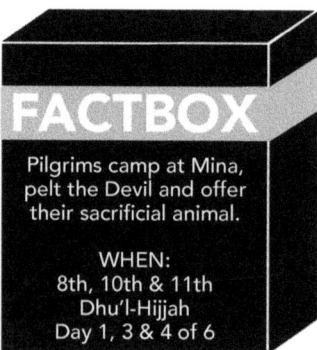

WHY DO PILGRIMS VISIT MINA?

Prophet Ibrahim عليه السلام had a dream in which he was commanded by Allah to sacrifice his son Isma'il عليه السلام. Dreams and visions of Prophets are considered to be commands from Allah. However, just before Prophet Ibrahim عليه السلام could sacrifice his son, Allah replaced Isma'il عليه السلام with a fine, white-horned ram from heaven. The reason why pilgrims visit Mina is because this is the place where Allah Most High sent the ram to Prophet Ibrahim عليه السلام as a ransom for his son.

WHY IS SHAYTAN PELTED?

Shaytan attempted to mislead the son of Prophet Ibrahim عليه السلام. When Prophet Ibrahim عليه السلام noticed this, he exclaimed "Allahu Akbar!" and pelted Shaytan using seven pebbles. This caused Shaytan to sink into the ground, and father and son proceeded further.

When the ground released him, Shaytan again attempted the same ploy. For the second time, Prophet Ibrahim عليه السلام pelted him, causing him to sink into the ground. When he again emerged from the ground, Shaytan made a third attempt, but Prophet Ibrahim عليه السلام dismissed him with another seven pebbles, while exclaiming, "Allahu Akbar!"

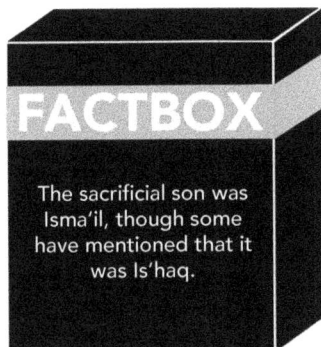

FACTBOX

The sacrificial son was Isma'il, though some have mentioned that it was Is'haq.

Each jamrah (stone pillar) represents each of Shaytan's attempts.

WHO WAS THE SACRIFICIAL SON: ISMA'IL OR IS'HAQ?

Commentators of the Quran have mentioned that it was Isma'il ﷺ who was ordered to be sacrificed, though some have mentioned that it was Is'haq ﷺ. Many earlier commentators, such as al-Tabari, take Is'haq ﷺ to be the son in question because of the Old Testament narrative, and also because the Quran is not explicit as to whether it was Isma'il or Is'haq.

However, several later commentators, such as al-Razi and Ibn Kathir, favour Isma'il ﷺ. Some of them go as far as to assert that the attribution to Is'haq ﷺ is derived from a corruption in the Bible. In short, the consensus is that the sacrificial son was Isma'il ﷺ.

> Then, when his son reached [the age of] running about with him, Prophet Ibrahim said: "My dear son, I dreamt that I must sacrifice you. Tell me what you think." The son replied: "Dear Father, do as you are ordered. If Allah chooses, you will find me among those who have patience."

REFERENCE: QURAN, SURAT AS-SAFFAT, 102
TRANSLATED BY: TAHIR MAHMOOD KIANI

WHY DO SCHOLARS BELIEVE ISMA'IL IS THE SACRIFICIAL SON?

The evidence of the sacrificial son being Isma'il ﷺ stems from the Quran:

Mention in the Book [the Quran] the story of Is-ma'il; he was true to his promise, a Messenger and a Prophet. He would order his people to worship God and pay the religious tax. His Lord was pleased with him.

REFERENCE: QURAN, SURAH MARYAM, 54-55
TRANSLATED BY: MUHAMMAD SARWAR

Furthermore, later commentators of the Quran believed the Old Testament was corrupted, hence they disregarded the Jewish narrative of Is'haq ﷺ being the sacrificial son. The corruption of the Jewish narrative stemmed from:

And He said, Take now thy son, thine "only" son Isaac...

REFERENCE: BIBLE (KING JAMES) VERSION, GENESIS 22:2

At no point was Is'haq ﷺ "the only son" of Ibrahim ﷺ because Isma'il ﷺ was the firstborn, and Prophet Ibrahim's "only son" for 14 years before Is'haq ﷺ was born. In short, several later commentators of the Quran believed Isma'il ﷺ was the sacrificial son because of a verse in the Quran, and because they deemed the Old Testament to be unreliable.

Also, in his *Mustadrak*, al-Hakim quotes Mu'awiyah ibn Abi Sufyan as saying:

We were with the Prophet (peace and blessings be upon him) when a Bedouin came to him and said: "O Messenger of Allah! I left behind me a barren and drought-stricken country. My property has vanished and my children are at loss. Bestow on me some of your favours, o Son of the The Two Sacrifices (adh-Dhabihayn) [Isma'il and 'Abdullah]." The Prophet (peace and blessings be upon him) smiled and did not rebuke him or deny the description.

Since the father of the Prophet Muhammad ﷺ survived the sacrifice in exchange for 100 camels, and his ancestor was Prophet Isma'il ﷺ (also known as a sacrifice), the Prophet ﷺ was thus known as the descendant of The Two Sacrifices.

WHAT ARE SOME DIFFERENCES BETWEEN THE MUSLIM AND JEWISH NARRATIVES?

One of the differences is that in the Quran, the son (whether it be Isma'il or Is'haq) is willing and aware of his sacrifice. In the Old Testament, Is'haq ﷺ is unaware of his sacrifice. A further difference pertains to the geographical location of the sacrifice whereby Muslims believe the sacrifice took place in Makkah, whilst Jews and Christians believe it took place in Jerusalem.

According to the Old Testament, the sacrifice occurred in Jerusalem because the Old Testament refers to Moriah as the mountain on which the Temple of Jerusalem is built.

> *... Take now thy son, thine only son Isaac, whom thou lovest, and get into the land of Moriah...*

REFERENCE: BIBLE (KING JAMES VERSION)
GENESIS 22:2

According to Islamic sources, the sacrifice occurred in Makkah [Mina] because the horns of the redemption sheep were once preserved inside the Ka'bah. The horns were later lost when the Ka'bah burned down in 63 AH/683 AD.

> *... I forgot to command you to cover up the two horns, for it is not appropriate that there be anything which distracts the worshipper while he is praying.*

REFERENCE: SUNAN ABU DAWUD
HADITH NUMBER: 2030, GRADED: HASAN

WHAT IS ARAFAT?

Arafat is an open and rugged plot of land that is situated approximately 13 miles (20 kilometres) to the southeast of Makkah. Staying at Arafat on the 9th of Dhu'l-Hijjah from midday to sunset is the essence of the Hajj. Arafat is among the sacred places where prayers are answered.

WHAT RITUALS TAKE PLACE AT ARAFAT?

One must be physically in Arafat for the obligation of this ritual to be fulfilled. It is recommended to spend every moment there in prayers and supplications, of which the following is recommended:

رَبَّنَا ظَلَمْنَا أَنْفُسَنَا وَإِن لَّمْ تَغْفِرْ لَنَا وَتَرْحَمْنَا لَنَكُونَنَّ مِنَ الْخَاسِرِينَ

Rabbanaa zalamnaa anfusanaa wa il'lam taghfir lanaa wa tarhamnaa lanakunanna minal khaasireen

Translation: "O our Lord! We have wronged our souls. And if You do not forgive us and have mercy on us, we shall certainly be amongst the losers."

REFERENCE: QURAN, SURAT AL-A'RAF, 23
TRANSLATED BY: DR. MUHAMMAD TAHIR-UL-QADRI

WHY IS IT CALLED ARAFAT?

One reason it is called Arafat is because it is the place where Prophet Adam عليه السلام reunited with Hawwa (Eve) عليها السلام after their descent from heaven, which had caused them to separate. Upon their arrival on earth, Prophet Adam عليه السلام descended in India, whilst Hawwa was in Arabia (Jeddah). Prophet Adam عليه السلام travelled to Arabia in search of the Ka'bah, and that is where he found Hawwa. Husband and wife recognised one another at Arafat, thus it became known as "a place where one recognises another".

Another reason it is called Arafat is because Allah sent Angel Jibril عليه السلام to Prophet Ibrahim عليه السلام and he performed Hajj for him, to teach him its rituals. When Prophet Ibrahim عليه السلام reached Arafat, he said: "'Araftu, 'araftu (I know, I know)." He had been to that area before. Thereafter, it was known as Arafat.

WHAT IS SPECIAL ABOUT THE DAY OF ARAFAT?

The Day of Arafat is the essence of Hajj and the single most important day. Being present at Arafat on 9th Dhu'l-Hijjah is the one rite that cannot be dispensed with or compensated. Anyone who misses this has compromised his or her Hajj.

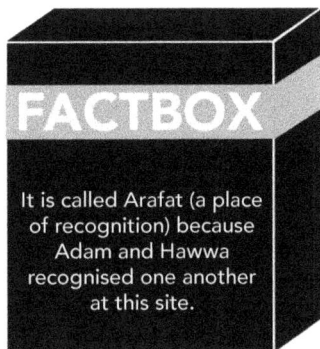

FACTBOX

It is called Arafat (a place of recognition) because Adam and Hawwa recognised one another at this site.

...The Hajj is Arafat, the Hajj is Arafat, the Hajj is Arafat...

REFERENCE: TIRMIDHI
HADITH NUMBER: 2975, GRADED: SAHIH

On this day, Allah majestically draws near and gazes upon his slaves and asks the Angels: "What do these people want?" So, you must humbly ask Him for whatever you want as this is a significant moment and a most blessed time.

...There is no day when Allah frees more slaves from the Fire than on the day of Arafat. He draws near, then He boasts about them before the Angels and asks: "What do these people want?"

REFERENCE: SAHIH MUSLIM
HADITH NUMBER: [3288] 436 – (1348)

Finally, standing on the plains of Arafat is a moment to reflect and ponder over one's life and spiritual wellbeing. It is an act of connecting with the Lord. Moreover, the meaning of the word "Arafat" and its historical connection with Prophet Adam ﷺ and Hawwa ought to be remembered in a manner that leads to the rekindling of the sacred bond that one only shares with one's spouse.

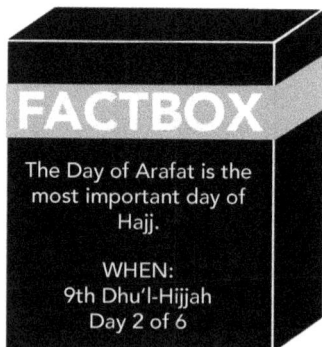

FACTBOX

The Day of Arafat is the most important day of Hajj.

WHEN:
9th Dhu'l-Hijjah
Day 2 of 6

... Allah says: "I am just as My slave thinks I am [i.e., I am Able to do for him what he thinks I can do for him], and I am with him if he re-

members Me. If he remembers Me in himself, I too, remember him in Myself; and if he remembers Me in a group of people, I remember him in a group that is better than them; and if he comes one span nearer to Me, I go one cubit nearer to him; and if he comes one cubit nearer to Me, I go a distance of two out-stretched arms nearer to him; and if he comes to Me walking, I go to him running."

REFERENCE: SAHIH AL-BUKHARI
HADITH NUMBER: 7405

The Day of Arafat is the essence of Hajj, and it is a day when Allah draws near in a manner that suits His majesty, and He forgives many. It is a day to reflect and offload to Allah. The historical meaning of the word Arafat and its connection with the reunion of Prophet Adam ﷺ and Hawwa ought to be pondered over in our own lives. There is no other day when Allah ransoms more slaves from the Fire and forgives than on the Day of Arafat.

Allah expresses His pride to His angels during the last part of the day on the Day of Arafat, about the people of Arafat. He says "Look at My slaves who have come unkempt and dusty."

Allah forgives those who spend the Day at Arafah.

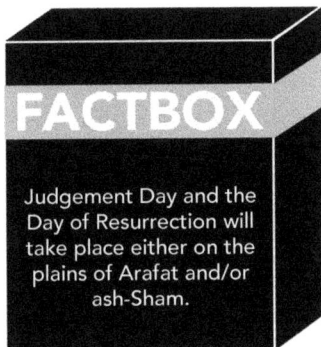

FACTBOX

Judgement Day and the Day of Resurrection will take place either on the plains of Arafat and/or ash-Sham.

A wide shot of the tent city set up in Mina, and below, a closer look at the tents just 2 kilometres from Makkah.

Mount Arafat is where Prophet Muhammad ﷺ delivered the Farewell Sermon.

WILL MANKIND BE RESURRECTED AT ARAFAT?

It is said that on the Day of Resurrection, mankind will be gathered on the plains of Arafat. Others say that mankind will be gathered in ash-Sham (modern day Syria, Palestine, Lebanon, Jordan, and parts of what is today Turkey).

The reason why people differ on whether mankind will be gathered in Arafat or ash-Sham (on the Day of Resurrection) is due to conflicting hadith evidence. Ibn 'Abbas ﷺ narrated that mankind will be gathered on the plains of Arafat. However, Ibn 'Umar ﷺ narrated that mankind will be gathered in ash-Sham.

> *Ibn 'Umar said that a freed slave girl of his came to him and said: "Times have become hard on me and I want to go to al-Iraq." He said: "Why not to ash-Sham, the land of resurrection?"...*

REFERENCE: TIRMIDHI
HADITH NUMBER: 3918, GRADED: SAHIH

To reconcile the two possibilities of whether mankind will be gathered at either Arafat or ash-Sham, some have suggested that it is possible that the area may span from Arafat to ash-Sham. This is probable, given the number of people, animals, and jinn that will be present at that time – exceeding billions.

Wherever the gathering place may be, standing on Mount Arafat during the Hajj is most certainly a glimpse of Judgement Day, considering the millions of pilgrims that jostle and gather there on the Day of Arafat. Lastly, it may not even be important "where" humanity gathers on the Day of Resurrection, because the Earth and its atmosphere will be destroyed and unrecognisable, so all land may even look similar. Allah knows best.

THE LAST SERMON OF PROPHET MUHAMMAD ﷺ

On the 9th of Dhu'l-Hijjah 10 AH [21st March 631 CE], on the Day of Arafat, Prophet Muhammad ﷺ remained inside his tent until the sun had set. He then ordered his she-camel to be readied. The camel was prepared. He proceeded down to a valley where 124,000–144,000 pilgrims were gathered. Here, he stood up and delivered his farewell speech.

Below is his blessed speech, which has been pieced together from various sources.

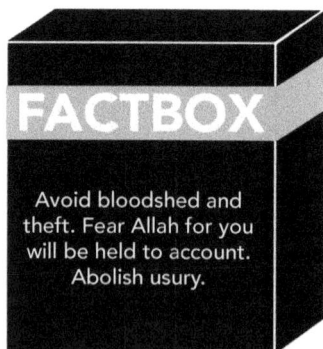

FACTBOX

Avoid bloodshed and theft. Fear Allah for you will be held to account. Abolish usury.

O people! Listen to my words. I do not know whether I shall ever meet you again in this place after this year. O people! Your blood and your property are sacrosanct until you meet your Lord, just as this day and this month of yours are sacred. Surely you will meet your Lord and He will question you about your deeds. I have [already] made this known. Let he who has a pledge return it to the one who entrusted him with it. All usury is abolished, but your capital belongs to you. Wrong not and you shall not be wronged. Allah has decreed that there will be no usury, and the usury of 'Abbas b. Abd al-Muttalib is abolished; all of it. All bloodshed in the pre-Islamic days is to be left unavenged. The first claim on blood I abolish is that of Rabi'a ibn al-Harith ibn 'Abd al-Muttalib (who was fostered among the Banu Layth and was killed by a man from the Hudhayl tribe). It is the first bloodshed in the pagan period which I deal with.

O people! Indeed, Shaytan has lost hope of ever being worshipped in this land of yours. But, if he can be obeyed in anything short of worship, he will be pleased in matters you minimise. So, remain wary of him in your religion. Postponement of a sacred month is only an excess of disbelief whereby those who disbelieve are misled; they allow it one year and forbid it another year. Time has completed its cycle and is as it was on the day that Allah created the heavens and earth. The number of months with Allah is twelve; four of them are sacred, three consecutive, and the Rajab of Mudar, which is between Jumada and Sha'ban.

FACTBOX

Be wary of Satan. Do not distort the calendars. Be kind to women.

Fear Allah regarding women, for they are your assistants. You have rights over your wives and they have rights over you. You have the right that they should not violate your bed and that they should not commit any open indecency. If they do, then Allah permits you to send them to separate rooms and to push them away, but not with harshness. If they refrain from these things, they have the right to their food and clothing with kindness. Treat women kindly, for they are entrusted with you and do not possess anything for themselves. You have taken them only as a trust from Allah, and you have made the enjoyment of their persons lawful by the Word of Allah, so you must understand and listen to my words, O men! For I have told you. Be kind with women, for you have taken them by Allah's covenant and earned the right to have sexual relations with them by Allah's Word.

I have conveyed the Message, and left with you something which, if you hold fast to it, you will never go astray: that is the Book of Allah and the Sunnah of His Prophet. For even if a slave was appointed over you, albeit an Ethiopian with a mutilated nose, and he rules with Allah's Book, then listen to him and obey. I do not want to see you after I am gone, reverting to disbelief, striking the necks of one another [killing each other].

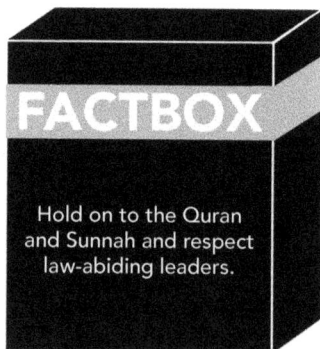

FACTBOX

Hold on to the Quran and Sunnah and respect law-abiding leaders.

O people! I am not succeeded by a prophet and you are not succeeded by any nation. Be mindful of your Lord, and pray your five [daily prayers], and fast your month [of Ramadan], and pay the Zakah on your wealth. I recommend you to perform the pilgrimage to the Sacred House of your Lord and obey those who are in charge of you. If so, you will enter the Paradise of your Lord.

Listen to my words, O people, for I have conveyed the Message and understand [it]. O people! You shall be asked about me, so what are you going to say? Know for certain that every Muslim is a brother of another Muslim, and that all Muslims are brethren. It is not lawful for a person [to take] from his brother except that which he has given him willingly, so do not wrong yourselves.

O people! Verily, your Lord is One and your forefather is one. Verily, there is no superiority of an Arab over a non-Arab or of a non-Arab over an Arab, or of a white person over a black person, or of a black person over a white person, except in terms of mindfulness of Allah [taqwa: piety and righteousness]. It is incumbent upon those who are present to inform those who are absent, in the hope that the absent might comprehend [what I have said] better than those who are present. Be witness, O Allah, that I have conveyed Your Message to Your people.

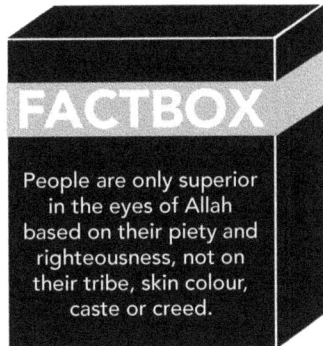

FACTBOX

People are only superior in the eyes of Allah based on their piety and righteousness, not on their tribe, skin colour, caste or creed.

After delivering this sermon, the Prophet Muhammad ﷺ recited the following Quranic verse (5:3):

Today, the disbelievers have given up all hope of [defeating] your religion, so don't be afraid of them but fear only Me. Today, I have made your religion perfect for you, completed My favour to you, and chosen Islam as the way of life for you.

SIGNIFICANCE OF THE LAST SERMON OF PROPHET MUHAMMAD ﷺ

The Last Sermon of the Prophet Muhammad ﷺ signifies a huge shift in culture, ethics, and socio-economic relations, as well as the promotion of human rights and equality among humanity. This sermon highlights, among other things:

- The right to one's reputation
- The right to security
- The right to own property
- The right to personal freedom
- The right to financial independence
- The right to reclaim a trust
- The right to access information
- The right to education
- The right to freedom from discrimination
- The rights of the spouses
- The right to equality in society
- The right to financial independence
- The right to freedom of religion
- The right to establish and maintain religious institutions

- The right to economic freedom
- The right to inheritance
- The right to justice

This is considered one of the earliest and most comprehensive declarations of human rights in history, addressed to thousands of witnesses on the plains of Arafat. The UN Declaration of Human Rights was not agreed upon, written, and adopted until 1948 CE, whereas the Magna Carta was written in 1215 CE. Additionally, John Locke discussed natural rights, referring to "life, liberty, and estate [property]" much later in the 17th century.

In the book *Furthering Human Rights* by C.G. Weeramantry, it is mentioned in the chapter titled "The Contribution of Islamic Jurisprudence to International Law and Human Rights":

> *We know also of Locke, the founding father of Western human rights, that he was a brilliant student at Oxford who played truant in regard to most of his lectures but that he assiduously attended only the lectures of Professor Pococke, the professor of Arabic studies. When Locke proclaimed his theory of inalienable rights and conditional rulership, this was new to the West, but could he not have had some glimmerings of this from his Arabic studies?*

In the same book is the following notable point:

> *We are constantly taught in law schools and international forums that the first systematic treatment of international law as a discipline was at the hands of Grotius with his famous Law of War and Peace in 1625. Rarely are we told, and few are*

the law teachers who are aware, that Mohammed bin Hasan Shaybani wrote an Introduction of the Law of Nations at the end of the eighth century, i.e. over 800 years earlier, and followed it with a second and more advanced treatise. Nor are we told that multi-volume treatises on the same subject followed within the next century or two.

WHAT IS MUZDALIFAH?

Muzdalifah is an open, rugged plot of land that is situated on the outskirts of Makkah, approximately 3 miles (almost 5 kilometres) from Arafat and from Mina. Pilgrims arrive at Muzdalifah from Arafat, and they stop and stay here for the whole night between the 9th and 10th days of Dhu'l-Hijjah, and this is where they combine the Maghrib and 'Isha ritual prayers.

Pilgrims also collect seven small stones at Muzdalifah to throw the next day at Jamrat al-'Aqabah (the large pillar) in Mina, or the full forty-nine to suffice the three days. For pelting the Jamrahs, pilgrims will need seven stones for 10th Dhu'l-Hijjah, twenty-one stones for 11th Dhu'l-Hijjah, and twenty-one stones for 12th Dhu'l-Hijjah.

WHY DO PILGRIMS VISIT MUZDALIFAH?

The reason pilgrims visit Muzdalifah is because this is the place where Prophet Adam ﷺ and Hawwa ﷺ drew close to one another. It is perhaps a moment to reflect in the presence of Allah the sacred bond that a husband and wife share. Moreover, its proximity to Mount Arafat is another reason for it being given this name.

As part of the Hajj rites, the Prophet Muhammad ﷺ stayed here overnight, reciting the Talbiyah, and he performed the Maghrib and 'Isha ritual prayers together. He rested until dawn the next day, led the Fajr ritual prayer, and mounted his camel, and set off for al-Mash'ar al-Haram, where he prayed and supplicated to Allah. He then collected seven stones and left for Mina before sunrise, reciting the Talbiyah throughout the journey.

Spending the night under the open sky with meagre possessions causes one to ponder over his own helplessness in this world as he is certain to leave it one day with nothing but the noble deeds he has done for the Hereafter. It is a reminder of our lack of true possessions and a mark of solidarity with the homeless. It also shows determination to carry out the will of Allah by collecting stones with the intention of pelting the Jamarah, as a symbol of thwarting Shaytan and rejecting his advances.

MISCELLANEOUS

HOW MANY TIMES DID THE PROPHET MUHAMMAD ﷺ PERFORM PILGRIMAGE?

After emigrating to Madinah, Prophet Muhammad ﷺ performed four 'Umrahs and one Hajj.

> *... The Prophet performed 'Umrah four times: i. 'Umrah from Hudaybiyyah, ii. 'Umrah the following year to make up for the one that was not completed previously, iii. the third 'Umrah from al-Ji'ranah, iv. the fourth that he performed with his Hajj.*

REFERENCE: MUSNAD AHMED
HADITH NUMBER: 2211
GRADED: SAHIH

The following table shows the dates Prophet Muhammad ﷺ performed 'Umrah and Hajj after emigrating to Madinah:

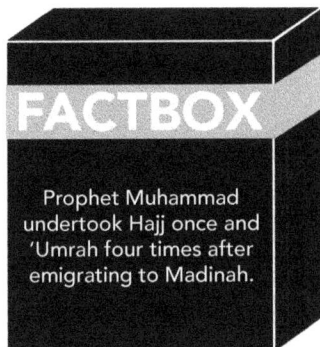

FACTBOX

Prophet Muhammad undertook Hajj once and 'Umrah four times after emigrating to Madinah.

NAME	HAJJ/ 'UMRAH	DATE
'Umrah of Hudaybiyyah	'Umrah	Dhu'l-Qa'dah 6 AH [628 CE]
'Umrat al-Qada'	'Umrah	Dhu'l-Qa'dah 7 AH [629 CE]
'Umrah from al-Ji'ranah	'Umrah	Dhu'l-Qa'dah 8 AH [630 CE]
Hajjat al-Wada'[11]	'Umrah & Hajj	Dhu'l-Hijjah 10 AH [632 CE]

In 6 AH, Prophet Muhammad ﷺ and his Companions set out from Madinah to perform 'Umrah but were halted at Hudaybiyyah and prevented from entering Makkah by the pagan authority. Following this, a peace treaty was agreed and signed at Hudaybiyyah between the Muslims and the pagans, whereby it was stipulated that the Muslims should, on that occasion, return to Madinah and come back the following year instead. Thus, at Hudaybiyyah, the Muslims removed their ihram, slaughtered their sacrificial animals and returned to Madinah. Although the Muslims were not able to perform 'Umrah on this occasion, they received the reward for it, hence it is considered an 'Umrah.

The 'Umrah which was performed the following year (according to the Hudaybiyyah Treaty), is known as 'Umrat al-Qada'. All of the Companions who were with the Prophet ﷺ on his previous journey to Hudaybiyyah and were still alive participated in this 'Umrah. Many other Muslims, apart from those Companions, also joined them. Two thousand Companions performed 'Umrah

---

11 *The History of al-Tabari, Vol. 9, The Last Years of the Prophet,* (1990), p.115.

with the Prophet ﷺ in Dhu'l-Qa'dah 7 AH. On his return from the battle of Hunayn, the Prophet ﷺ stayed at a place called al-Ji'ranah and distributed the booty among the fighters. From there, he entered into the state of ihram and performed 'Umrah. This 'Umrah was performed in 8 AH.

The Prophet ﷺ performed the fourth 'Umrah with his Hajj. He started his journey in the last days of the month of Dhu'l-Qa'dah and completed his 'Umrah on the 4th of Dhu'l-Hijjah in the year 10 AH.

Furthermore, there is some questionable evidence which suggests the Prophet ﷺ performed Hajj three times in total: twice before he emigrated to Madinah, and once after the Migration. It is uncertain if he actually did perform Hajj prior to his fourteenth year of Prophethood (i.e. 12/13 September 622 CE) which was the day of migration to Madinah. If he did, it is also unknown if it was before or after declaring Prophethood.

> *... The Messenger of Allah performed Hajj three times; twice before he emigrated, and once after he had emigrated to Madinah....*
>
> REFERENCE: SUNAN IBN MAJAH
> HADITH NUMBER: 3076, GRADED: DA'IF

In short, it can be said with certainty that Prophet Muhammad ﷺ performed Hajj once and 'Umrah on four occasions after he emigrated to Madinah. He may also have performed Hajj a few times before he emigrated to Madinah and prior to announcing Prophethood. However, the Hajj was not obligated until after the Hijrah (Migration) to Madinah. Allah knows best.

DID PREVIOUS PROPHETS VISIT MAKKAH?

Yes. The Prophets from among the descendants of Prophet Ya'qub ﷺ also used to visit Makkah for Hajj, even though their qiblah (direction for ritual prayer) was Bayt al-Maqdis.

> ... We were with the Messenger of Allah between Makkah and Madinah, and we passed through a valley. He said: "What valley is this?" They said: "Azraq Valley." He said: "It is as if I can see Musa..." Then we travelled on until we came to a narrow pass, and he said: "What pass is this?" They said: "Thaniyyat Harsha" or "Laft." He said: "It is as if I can see Yunus ... passing through this valley, reciting the Talbiyah."

REF: SUNAN IBN MAJAH
HADITH NUMBER: 2891
GRADED: SAHIH

It was narrated that 'Abdullah ibn 'Abbas said: "The Prophets used to enter the al-Haram walking barefoot. They would circumambulate the House and complete all the rituals barefoot and walking."

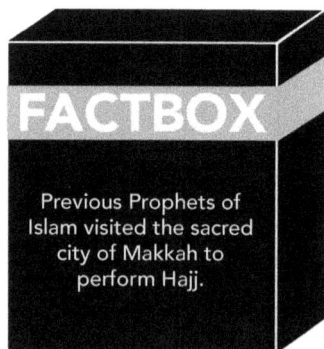

Prophet 'Isa ﷺ will also perform the pilgrimage:

Hanzala al-Aslami reported: "I heard Abu Hurayrah narrating from the Holy Prophet who said, 'I

FACTBOX

Previous Prophets of Islam visited the sacred city of Makkah to perform Hajj.

swear by the One in Whose control is my life! Ibn Maryam [Jesus] would certainly pronounce the Talbiyah for Hajj or for 'Umrah or for both [together as in Hajj Qir'an] in the valley of Rawha.'"

AVOID CONFLICT IN DHU'L-HIJJAH AND MAKKAH

Conflicts are always prohibited, but even more so in the Month of Pilgrimage (Dhu'l-Hijjah), as it is a sacred month. This prohibition in Dhu'l-Hijjah predates Islam – even the Arabs of the past would honour it. This prohibition [to avoid conflict] in the month of Dhu'l-Hijjah is still in place, so long as the enemy respects the sanctity of the month and does not engage in armed conflict.

They ask you about concerning fighting in the Sacred Month. Reply: "It is a big crime to fight in it."

REFERENCE: QURAN
SURAT AL-BAQARAH, 217

... If someone attacks you then you may fight back equal to how he attacked you, but you must continue to be mindful of Allah and know that He is with those who are mindful [of Him].

REFERENCE: QURAN
SURAT AL-BAQARAH, 194

FACTBOX

The month of Dhu'l-Hijjah and the city of Makkah is a sacred time and place in which conflict is prohibited.

Furthermore, after the Conquest of Makkah, Prophet Muhammad ﷺ forbade all armed confrontation in the city.

Nevertheless, throughout history, the sanctity of Dhu'l-Hijjah and of Makkah has been frequently violated despite the religious restrictions that are in place to avoid conflict.

> *... Makkah has been made sacred by Allah, not by the people. It is not permissible for any person who believes in Allah and the Last Day to shed blood in it, or to cut its trees. If anyone seeks permission to fight in it because the Messenger of Allah fought in it, say to him: Allah allowed His Messenger [to fight therein] but He did not allow you...*

REFERENCE: SUNAN AL-NASA'I
HADITH NUMBER: 2879, GRADED: SAHIH

PILGRIMS ARE GUESTS OF ALLAH

Pilgrims are guests of Allah who have arrived by invitation from Him:

> *... The pilgrim performing Hajj and 'Umrah are a delegation to Allah. He invited them, so they responded to Him, and they ask Him and He gives to them.*

REFERENCE: SUNAN IBN MAJAH
HADITH NUMBER: 2893, GRADED: HASAN

It can also be said that pilgrims are responding to the call of Prophet Ibrahim ﷺ:

*And call the people to Hajj, and they shall come
to you on foot and mounted on every lean camel –
coming from every faraway route.*

REFERENCE: QURAN, SURAT AL-HAJJ, 27

PILGRIMAGE IS JIHAD FOR WOMEN

Pilgrimage for women has been described as jihad,
which literally means "to strive" or "to exert to the ut-
most".[12] Jihad has two main connotations: "the lesser
jihad" which is to physically fight, and "the greater jihad"
which is the inner struggle against the self.[13] Jihad for
men is generally understood in the context of warfare;
but for women, Hajj is a form of jihad because of the
arduous journey and living conditions experienced by
pilgrims in Makkah and its surrounding areas.

> ... *"O Messenger of Allah, is jihad obligatory for
> women?" He said: "Yes: Upon them is a jihad in
> which there is no fighting: Hajj and 'Umrah."*

REFERENCE: SUNAN IBN MAJAH
HADITH NUMBER: 2901, GRADED: SAHIH

CAN HAJJ BE DONE ON SOMEONE ELSE'S BEHALF?

Yes. Since Hajj is a duty one "owes" to Allah, this "debt"
can be paid off by anyone who is willing to pay, whether
for themselves or for someone else.

---

12 *English Translation of Jami At-Tirmidhi, Vol.6,* p.587.
13 *A Glossary of Islamic Terms,* p.213.

... Pilgrimage to this House, for those who can perform it, is a duty upon people to Allah... .

REFERENCE: QURAN, SURAT AL-IMRAN, 97

... "My father is an old man and cannot ride. May I perform Hajj on his behalf?" He ﷺ said: "Yes, because if your father owed a debt, you would pay it off."

REFERENCE: SUNAN IBN MAJAH
HADITH NUMBER: 2909, GRADED: SAHIH

WHAT IF SOMEONE DIES DURING HAJJ?

If one dies during Hajj, it is a blessing, because you will be raised on the Day of Resurrection saying: "Labbayk!"

Allah says: "And if anyone leaves his home in search of the pleasure of Allah and His Messenger, and then death overtakes him – his reward from Allah is already guaranteed. Allah is always Most Forgiving, Ever-Merciful."

REFERENCE: QURAN, SURAH AN-NISA, 100

And the Holy Prophet ﷺ said: "Whoever travels in the path of Allah while cherishing firmly the intention to seek the pleasure of Allah, and then death overtakes him, he is a martyr."

Ibn 'Abbas reported: "A man who was performing the ritual of standing on the plains of Arafat in the company of the Holy Prophet ﷺ fell from his mount and was crushed to death by the beast. Then, the

Holy Prophet ﷺ told his companions: 'Wash him…
and shroud him in two pieces [of cloth] and do not
cover his head, for he will be raised up making the
chant of Talbiyah on the Day of Resurrection."

REFERENCE: SAHIH AL-BUKHARI
HADITH NUMBER: 1266, GRADED: SAHIH

COMPARISON BETWEEN THE HAJJ OF THE POLYTHEIST AND OF THE MUSLIM

During the Jahiliyyah (Age of Ignorance) up until the Conquest of Makkah by Prophet Muhammad ﷺ, the polytheists across Arabia would visit Makkah to circumambulate and venerate the Ka'bah, and to purchase and pay homage to idols. However, the monotheistic religion preached by the Holy Prophet Muhammad ﷺ sought to do away with the sin of polytheism by removing the idols that were housed inside the Ka'bah in particular. The faith of the Holy Prophet ﷺ threatened the livelihood and economy of Makkah because it discredited the idols, which the pagans would not only worship but also purchase.

After suffering years of hardship at the hands of the polytheist establishment in Makkah, Prophet Muhammad ﷺ and the early Muslims found a new abode and emigrated to Madinah. A bitter civil war ensued in the Arabian peninsula (from September 622 CE to January 630 CE)[14] between the Muslims, now in Madinah, against the polytheists of Makkah. This war ended with the Conquest of Makkah by Prophet Muhammad ﷺ and the destruction of all 360 idols that were housed inside the

---

14 Ar-Raheequl Makhtum (The Sealed Nectar), p.392.

Ka'bah, after which the polytheists were barred from performing Hajj and polytheism was abolished in Arabia.

Below is a brief comparison between the rituals of Hajj as performed by the polytheists and the Muslims.

RITUAL	POLYTHEIST PRACTICE/BELIEF	MUSLIM PRACTICE/BELIEF
'Umrah	Sinful to perform 'Umrah during Hajj.[15]	Acceptable to perform Hajj Tamattu' – 'Umrah in the same journey as Hajj.
Talbiyah	Here we are, You have no partner, except a partner that You have, and You control him and all that he possesses.[16]	Here I am at your service, O Allah, here I am. Here I am. No partner do You have. Truly, the praise and favour are Yours, and the dominion. No partner do You have.[17]
Tawaf	Some pilgrims wore clothes, others did not.[18]	All pilgrims wear clothes.
Sa'y	Some pilgrims performed the Sa'y,[19] others did not.[20]	All pilgrims perform the Sa'y.

15 English Translation of Sunan Abu Dawud, Vol. 2, p.365.
16 Muslim, Sahih, Hadith 1185.
17 Muslim, Sahih, Hadith 1184.
18 Al-Bukhari, Sahih, Hadith 1665.
19 Muslim, Sahih, Hadith 1277.
20 Muslim, Sahih, Hadith 1277.

RITUAL	POLYTHEIST PRACTICE/BELIEF	MUSLIM PRACTICE/BELIEF
Arafat	Pilgrims from Makkah stayed at Muzdalifah.	All pilgrims stay at Arafat.
	Pilgrims from outside of Makkah stayed at Arafat.[21]	
Muzdalifah	Pilgrims leave after sunrise.[22]	Pilgrims leave before sunrise.

WHAT WAS THE FUNDAMENTAL DIFFERENCE BETWEEN THE PILGRIMAGE OF THE POLYTHEISTS AND MUSLIMS?

Originally, Makkah was a monotheistic city founded by Hajar صلى الله عليه وسلم, and the Ka'bah was built by Prophet Ibrahim صلى الله عليه وسلم and Isma'il صلى الله عليه وسلم to worship Allah alone. However, with the passage of time, idolatry was introduced into Makkan society from Syria.[23] After the introduction of idols, Makkah and the Ka'bah became a centre and symbol of polytheism. Interestingly, the form of polytheism that developed in Makkah was one infused with aspects of Abrahimic monotheism, whereby the pagans believed in Allah and knew of Isma'il صلى الله عليه وسلم, yet they also believed in other entities as gods.

---

21 English Translation of Jami At-Tirmidhi, Vol.2, pp.295–296.
22 English Translation of Sunan Ibn Majah, Vol.4, (2007), pp.192–193.
23 Ar-Raheequl Makhtum (The Sealed Nectar), p.34.

Monotheism: The belief that there is only one God.

Polytheism: The worship of or belief in more than one god.

REFERENCE: COLLINS DICTIONARY

In short, the fundamental difference between polytheist-pagans of Arabia who believed they were upon the religion of Prophet Ibrahim ﷺ, and later monotheist-Muslims who also believed they were upon the religion of Prophet Ibrahim ﷺ, was "intention and reverence" towards either "idols" or "Allah alone" in acts of ritual worship pertaining to the Hajj.

CONCLUSION

Hajj is to undertake a pilgrimage to Makkah. It is a pilgrimage that mankind owes to Allah, in which pilgrims respond to a call that Prophet Ibrahim ﷺ made, a call that he made upon completing the construction of the Ka'bah thousands of years ago. There are three types of Hajj, and the commonality they share is that they all include the acts of 'Umrah. 'Umrah is a ritual in the month of Hajj that Prophet Muhammad ﷺ introduced and is known as Hajj Tamattu'. Hajj is to circumambulate the Ka'bah and visit various landmarks in remembrance of Allah and in commemoration of past events.

The many rituals of Hajj are carried out in the space of five to six days. These rituals primarily involve visiting the landmarks of Mina, Arafat, Muzdalifah, and, of course, the Ka'bah. The most important day of Hajj is the Day of Arafat because it is the day on which Allah draws near and asks the angels, "What do these people want?" On this day, pilgrims ask for forgiveness of all sins and blessings in their lives and in the Hereafter, praying for themselves, their loves ones, and the entire ummah.

During the month of Hajj, the city of Makkah is abuzz with pilgrims from across the world, all of whom dress in similar clothes and chant the Talbiyah. The pilgrims circumambulate the Ka'bah, a sanctuary initially built by angels for Prophet Adam ﷺ and later rediscovered by Prophet Ibrahim ﷺ approximately 4,000 years ago. Pilgrims gather around a corner of the Ka'bah in which there is a black stone, al-Hajar al-Aswad, which absorbs the sins of those that kiss it, touch it, or indicate towards it. This stone will come alive on the Day of Resurrection and ask Allah to forgive the sins that it holds.

In close proximity to the Ka'bah are two mounts named Safa and Marwah. Male pilgrims run and walk, while female pilgrims only walk, between these two hills in remembrance of Lady Hajar's ﷺ quest for water when she was left alone in the wilderness by Prophet Ibrahim ﷺ by Divine Command. She ran between Safa and Marwah in search of help to quench the thirst of baby Isma'il ﷺ. Help eventually came by way of an angel that struck the ground, forming the Zamzam spring (which later became a well) and the city of Makkah was established in the time of Prophet Ibrahim ﷺ. The discovery of the Zamzam well later attracted the Jurhum tribe who settled there, which allowed Makkah to expand. Prophet Ibrahim ﷺ later returned to Makkah to rebuild the Ka'bah with Isma'il ﷺ and made an attempt to sacrifice his son Isma'il through the Divine Decree of Allah, which was a test of faith for Prophet Ibrahim ﷺ and his family.

Hajj also includes visiting Mina, Arafat, and Muzdalifah to remind the pilgrims of pivotal moments in human history, and to reflect upon our own lives and call upon Allah's favour and mercy. At the same time we must accept "what is in His hands are all aspects of life, from the past to the present and beyond, including the good and bad, and He knows what is best for us and does not burden a soul with grief or insecurity, except what He knows we can handle. He gave us experiences to be happy, and moments of hardship to build character; all accumulating into thoughts and memories that are to be utilised as a catalyst towards His remembrance, and aid us in our journey towards Jannah." You may ask Allah for whatever you want at Arafat, but ultimately it is best to ask Him to do whatever He knows is best for us.

Lastly, Hajj is also fondly remembered for the Last Sermon of Prophet Muhammad ﷺ in which over 100,000 pilgrims gathered on the plains of Arafat to participate with the Prophet ﷺ in his Farewell Pilgrimage. He ﷺ spoke of the importance of equality among mankind, and the importance of fairness and justice in the treatment of women. He also spoke of other matters of importance pertaining to unity and remaining steadfast in religion. Previous Prophets had performed Hajj in Makkah, as did the pagans; but Prophet Muhammad ﷺ showed Muslims a way of carrying out the rituals in a manner that was somewhat similar to others yet unique in many aspects.

May Allah give us all the opportunity to make the journey of Hajj and accept it from us. Ameen.

BIBLIOGRAPHY

Afsaruddin, A. (2018, October 30). Umar I. Retrieved May 20, 2019, from Encyclopaedia Britannica: https://www.britannica.com/biography/Umar-I

Al-Bukhari, M. I.-I. (1997). In M. M. Khan, S. N. Al-Ubaydi, M. H. Nasr, M.-u.-D. Al-Hilali, & M. H. As-Sudani (Eds.), *The Translation of the Meanings of Sahih Al-Bukhari Arabic-English* (2nd ed.). Riyadh, Saudi Arabia: Maktaba Dar-us-Salam.

Al-Hajjaj, I. A. (2007). In H. A. Zai, A. Khaliyl, & N. al-Khattab (Eds.), *English Translation of Sahih Muslim* (First ed.). Riyadh: Maktaba Dar-us-Salam.

Ali, A. Y. (1989). In I. C. The Presidency of Islamic Researches (Ed.), *The Holy Quran - English translation of the Meanings and Commentary*. Al-Medina Al-Munawarah: King Fahd Holy Quran Printing Complex.

Al-Mubarakpuri, S.-R. (1996). In A. Mujahid (Ed.), *Ar-Raheequl Makhtum (The Sealed Nectar), Biography of the Noble Prophet* (First ed.). Riyadh: Dar-us-Salam.

Al-Qazwini, I. M. (2007). In H. A. Zai, N. al-Khattab, A. Khaliyl, & H. Khattab (Eds.), *English Translation of Sunan Ibn Majah* (First ed.). Riyadh: Maktaba Dar-us-Salam.

al-Tabari, A. J. (1990). *The History of al-Tabari - Volume 9 - The Last Years of the Prophet.* In I. Abbas, C. E. Bosworth, J. Lassner, F. Rosenthal, & E. Yar-Shater (Eds.). New York, New York, United States of America: State University of New York Press.

al--Nasa'i, I. H. (2007). In H. A. Zai, H. Khattab, A. Khaliyl, & N. al-Khattab (Eds.), *English Translation of Sunan An-Nasai* (First ed., p.52,

Vol. 3). Riyadh: Maktaba Dar-us-Salam.

al-Nasa'i, I. H. (2007). *English Translation of Sunan An-Nasai.* In H. A. Zai, H. Khattab, & A. Khaliyl (Eds.), *English Translation of Sunan An-Nasai* (N. al-Khattab, Trans., First ed., Vol.3). Riyadh, Saudi Arabia: Maktaba Dar-us-Salam.

Ashath, I. H. (2008). In H. A. Zai, Y. Qadhi, A. Khaliyl, & A. M. Mujahid (Eds.), *English Translation of Sunan Abu Dawud* (First ed.). Riyadh: Maktaba Dar-us-Salam.

Al-Shaybani, A. A. (2012). In H. Al-Khattab, Darussalam, & N. Al-Khattab (Eds.), *English Translation of Musnad Imam Ahmed Bin Hanbal* (First ed.). Riyadh, Saudi Arabia: Maktaba Dar-us-Salam.

Al-Tirmidhi, I. H. (2007). In H. A. Zai, A. Khaliyl, Islamic Research Section Darussalam, & A. M. Mujahid (Eds.), *English Translation of Jami At-Tirmidhi* (A. Khaliyl, Trans., First ed.). Riyadh: Maktaba Dar-us-Salam.

Bewley, A. (1998). In Bookwork Norwich (Ed.), *A Glossary of Islamic Terms* (p.23, p.69). London: Ta-Ha Publishers.

biblegateway.com. (2016, March 27). Retrieved from https://www.biblegateway.com/

Dukes, K. (n.d.). English Translation. Retrieved May 10, 2019, from The Quranic Arabic Corpus: http://corpus.quran.com/translation.jsp

Hashmi, T., & Malik, A. (2011). *Hajj & Umrah Made Easy.* In S. Hasan (Ed.). Birmingham, United Kingdom: Al-Hidaayah Publishing & Distribution.

Ishaq, I. (2004). In A. Guillaume (Ed.), *The Life of Muhammad A Translation of Ibn Ishaq's Sirat Rasul Allah.* Karachi: Oxford University Press.

IslamiCity: Hijri-Gregorian Converter. (n.d.). Retrieved October 8, 2017, from IslamiCity: http://www.islamicity.org/hijri-gregorian-converter/?AspxAutoDetectCookieSupport=1#

Kathir, I. (2003). In S.-R. Al-Mubarakpuri (Ed.), *Tafsir Ibn Kathir* (Abridged) (Second ed.). Riyadh: Maktaba Dar-us-Salam.

Kiani, Tahir Mahmood (2022), *The Easy Quran.* London: Ta-Ha Publishers Ltd.

Mubarakpuri, S.-R. (2002). *History of Mecca.* Riyadh: Darussalam.

S. H. Nasr, C. K. Dagli, M. M. Dakake, & J. E. Lumbard (Eds.), (2015). *The Study Quran* (First ed.). New York: Harper Collins.

Smith, S. (2015, September 16). BBC News. Retrieved April 11, 2021, from Science & Environment: https://www.bbc.co.uk/news/science-environment-34170798

Sunnah.com, for the retrieval of hadiths from al-Bukhari, Muslim, al-Nasa'i, Abu Dawud, al-Tirmidhi, Ibn Majah, Ahmad, and others, April-May, 2024.

Tahir-ul-Qadri, Shaykh Dr. Muhammad (2013). In M. Naz, M. Rana, M. I. Sulaiman, & W. A. Amin (Eds.), *Mawlid Al-Nabi Celebration and Permissibility* (First ed.). London, England: Minhaj-ul-Quran.

Tahir-ul-Qadri, Shaykh Dr. Muhammad (2015). altafsir.com. (Royal Aal al-Bayt Institute for Islamic Thought) Retrieved from altafsir.com: http://www.altafsir.com/ViewTranslations.asp?Display=yes&SoraNo=35&Ayah=32&toAyah=32&Language=2&LanguageID=2&TranslationBook=21

The Editors of *Encyclopaedia Britannica*. (2013, November 1). Akedah. Retrieved April 27, 2021, from Encyclopaedia Britannica: https://www.britannica.com/topic/Akedah

www.ingramcontent.com/pod-product-compliance
Lightning Source LLC
Chambersburg PA
CBHW042339040426
42448CB00019B/3337